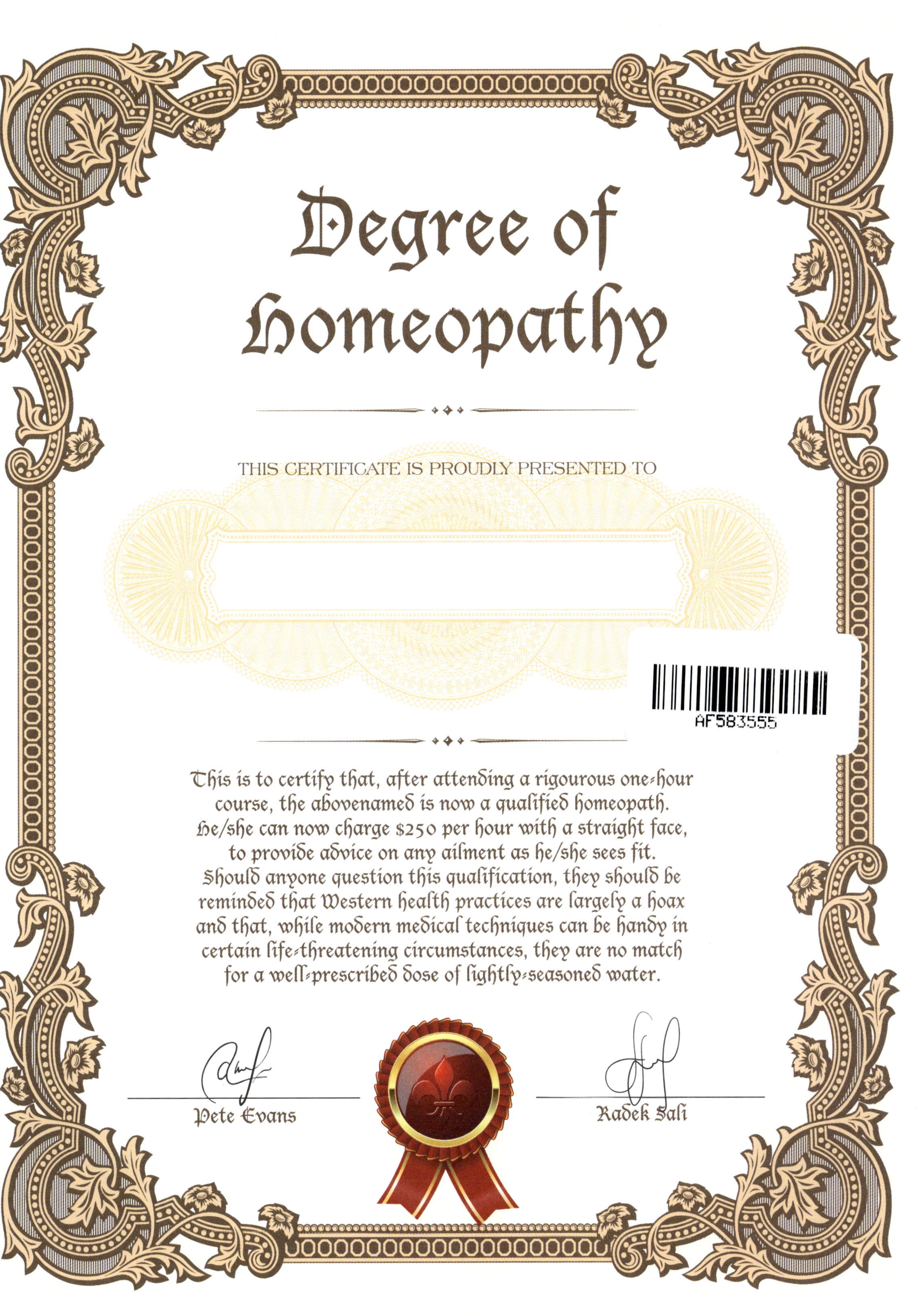

Degree of Homeopathy

THIS CERTIFICATE IS PROUDLY PRESENTED TO

This is to certify that, after attending a rigourous one-hour course, the abovenamed is now a qualified homeopath. He/she can now charge $250 per hour with a straight face, to provide advice on any ailment as he/she sees fit. Should anyone question this qualification, they should be reminded that Western health practices are largely a hoax and that, while modern medical techniques can be handy in certain life-threatening circumstances, they are no match for a well-prescribed dose of lightly-seasoned water.

Pete Evans

Radek Sali

Welcome nonbelievers

Welcome to the second edition of the Anti-Experts guide to Everything - they said an entire magazine should never be printed on 100% recycled untreated toilet paper, but we sure showed them!

You may well ask what the need is to print a second edition of the Anti-Experts guide, only two years after the first one cured all medical problems and solved global warming forever with our ingenious 'clean coal' idea, but the answer is quite simple. Unfortunately every single person who owned the first edition has now died of easily preventable diseases. I think we can all see the pattern here, and clearly this is some kind of attempt by the government to assassinate us Anti-Vaxers before our message becomes too popular.

So what has changed since we published the last edition two years ago? Well for one thing, the Coronavirus is now devastating the world. We only hope medical science is able to find the right crystal to cure the disease in time.

Also Australia has suffered its worst bushfire season on record. Unlike some who claim it was 'global warming' that caused the fires, we know all too well that this is simply the work of the Greens activists, who famously love destroying bushland and killing animals. We have reason to believe these are the very same Greens arsonists who are also responsible for melting the ice caps, bleaching the barrier reef, and pouring 12000 gallons of crude oil into the Mexican gulf. What monsters.

In any case, we're back, except for Geoff who died after an unfortunate yet unpreventable bout of polio.

So sit back, strap on your foil hat, pour yourself a nice warm glass of snake oil, and let's explore all the secret truths doctors don't want you to know, simply because they'll do 'irreparable damage to your health'.

All Hail Tom Cruise,
Charles Firth
MANAGING EDITOR

Who to blame

Writers
James Schloeffel
Charles Firth
Cam Smith
Andrew Hansen
Dom Knight
Shane Cubis
Rohan Arneil
Stephen Lacey
Ben Keating
David Piepers
James Cavahl

Subscriptions
subscriptions@chaser.com.au
Phone: 02 8227 6486
Fax: 02 8227 6410
Address: PO Box 161
Hornsby NSW 2077

Design
Michelle Turcsanyi

Editor
Cam Smith

Managing Editor
Charles Firth

16

The Chaser's Disclaimer Managing editor: Charles Firth. This is the nineteenth issue of *The Chaser Quarterly*, and is published by Chaser Quarterly Pty Ltd (ACN 141758812) of 270/398-408 Pitt St Sydney. While effort has been made to verify any facts contained within this publication, no responsibility will be taken for errors or omissions contained herein by Chaser Quarterly Pty Ltd, its officers, employees or their agents. Readers should rely on their own enquiries when making decisions touching on their interests. Apart from satirical articles which discuss public figures for the purposes of humour, any mention of any person, alive or dead, is entirely coincidental. We expect readers to use their own common sense in determining the truth or otherwise of any statement in this publication. *The Chaser Quarterly* is available in newsagents and bookshops across Australia, and is printed by Spotpress, 24-26 Lilian Fowler Pl, Marrickville, NSW, 2204. Subscribe at **chasershop.com** and stay up to date at **chaser.com.au**

100% WATER

THE STRONGEST ALCOHOL ON THE MARKET

Excess consumption may cause drowning.
May contain traces of dihydrogen monoxide.

DRINK RESPONSIBLY

We are facing global catastrophe and collapse, and it's all caused by one thing...

We are on the verge of a global catastrophe. It affects us all, and not just us, but our children and our children's children. If we're honest, this global catastrophe is something we've known about for along time, and we're just not doing enough to stop it. And it's getting worse.

I'm talking, of course about experts. They're everywhere. You go to the mechanic and suddenly HE'S the expert in brake pads.

You go to the hospital, and suddenly the lady with the "medical degree" and the "ten years of post-graduate study" knows more about my genital warts than me.

You hop on a plane, and only people with the correct "qualifications" are allowed to fly the plane (unless you're travelling Jetstar).

What about my opinion on your pneumonia? Why can't I express my opinion on how to construct a national electricity grid? Why do I need certifications to conduct safety repairs on high occupancy mass transit vehicles?

Luckily, across the Western world, people are fighting back.

In the USA, Donald Trump is leading the way. It's a victory for the ordinary working voter. What better way to give the middle finger to the experts on Wall Street than to elect someone who owns a building on the middle of Wall Street?

And over the UK, Boris Johnson has proven that with a bit of hard work and determination, anyone who has been to Eton can become Prime Minister. It's the British dream.

And even here in coal country, Scott Morrison is proving that you don't need fancy degrees, or even a functioning moral core, to run this country. Scott Morrison's Australia is based on the very simple principle of selling out Australia to the highest bidder, and it doesn't an expert to do that.

Anyway, I've got to go. Coronavirus is shaping up to be a real national emergency, so I'm doing a ScoMo and lying low in Hawaii for a few weeks. See you when I get back (if you survive).

WANT TO BE AS RICH AS I AM?

THEN GRAB A TICKET TO MY 3 DAY INTENSIVE SEMINAR 'HOW TO GET RICH TRICKING IDIOTS INTO BUYING TICKETS TO A GET RICH QUICK SEMINAR'. IT WORKED FOR ME, AND IT COULD WORK FOR YOU TOO!

Only a year ago i was a poor university dropout with a string of failed businesses to my name. But now, thanks to the power of positive thought, and the even greater power of idiots buying my get rich quick books, I'm a multi-millionaire with my own yacht!

So how can you harness the power of idiots buying books to make a fortune? Those answers and more are revealed in the 12 editions of my new book - on sale now for just $69.99 per copy, plus tax.

LESSONS INCLUDE:

- Where to buy oversized 80s headset microphones

- The perfect $12 white to match with your blazer

- How to convince a rich person to let you pose on their yacht for your marketing photoshoot, AND

- All the best countries to lay low in once your followers realise they've been conned

Ten celebrities who were vaccinated and later died

The poisonous ingredients found in vaccinations don't discriminate. Here are five well-known personalities who were vaccinated and died.

John F. Kennedy

PRESIDENT President Kennedy famously died of a head-shot wound in 1963, but conspiracy theorists have always suggested there may be more to the story. Was the shooting organised by the CIA to cover up the fact that Kennedy was vaccinated? We made a FOI request to get to the bottom of the case, but were rejected on the grounds of 'wasting government time' which seems awfully convenient, doesn't it?

Princess Diana

ROYALTY Everyone remembers the images of the car crash, but most have forgotten the much earlier pictures of baby Diana getting her diphtheria jab. A life tragically cut short by immunisation.

Steve Irwin

AUSSIE Stabbed in the heart by a stingray at the age of 44, and stabbed in the arm at six months by a vaccination needle. I think we all know which one caused the Aussie icon's death.

Michael Jackson

ICON When Michael Jackson said millions of children suffer around the world needlessly, he was referring, of course, to needles. Jackson himself recieved a Hepatitis B injection in 1962 and less than 50 years later he was dead in what the autopsy has reported as the result of medical malpractice. I think we can all read between the lines there.

Amy Winehouse

MUSICIAN Addicted to a range of vaccinations, Winehouse managed to escape Hepatitis A, Hepatitis B and acellular pertussis, but couldn't escape death. What a waste.

IRWIN: PHOTO BY JUSTIN SULLIVAN/GETTY IMAGES; MICHAEL JACKSON: KEVIN MAZUR/WIREIMAGE/GETTY IMAGES; WINEHOUSE: PAUL BERGEN/REDFERNS/GETTY IMAGES.

Paul McCartney

BEATLE One of the most famous and influential musicians of the 20th century, Paul McCartney was replaced by a lookalike in the late 60s after he died of a flu injection.

The Queen Mother

DRUNK With a life cut short at the tragically young age of 101, this poor innocent woman could have been expected to live at least another 200 years had it not been for the anti-malarial properties of the 12 gin and tonics she drank every day.

Bob Dylan

MUSICIAN Though not technically dead, his career and legacy both went terminal the day the famous folk singer decided to get a Hep C booster.

THE CORPSE OF BOB DYLAN IS SO WELL PRESERVED IT'S ALMOST LIFELIKE

Jesus

H. CHRIST He could save humanity, but he couldn't save himself from the tetanus shots required after getting a rusty nail in his hand, hand, foot and other foot.

You

RIP We were going to have a mirror here but it was too expensive so instead here's a grey box where you can draw yourself.

Tamám Shud Man

SPY Found alone and without identification wearing a suit passed away on a popular beach, the only clue we have to this man's untimely death is the fact that he was probably vaccinated in order to silence whatever secrets he knew.

Advertiser-supported content
If you're wanting to be paid for your content, think about writing advertiser-supported content. All it costs is your integrity. Cheap!

Modern journalism is all about having another source of income to rely on. Whether it's dealing drugs, prostitution, or, worst of all, writing for News Corp, success requires you to diversify away from the one thing that is now proven to not make any money: journalism. Nowadays being a 'journalist' mainly involves re-writing Wikipedia, and passing on information you read somewhere else. Anyway, you've racked up the HELP debt for that Bachelor of Journalism or whatever, so you may as well make the most of it.

How to write a balanced article (balance an expert with an idiot)

Unless you're being paid to write an op-ed column, your articles must be as exquisitely balanced as the scales of justice. It's vitally important to show both sides of the story, no matter how obvious the 'correct' side is. You are a dispassionate recorder of current events. This means that if you ask a so-called expert for their view on a given topic, you have to ask an idiot too.

It sounds like hard work, but don't worry. As soon as you start sharing your published pieces on social media, the idiots will contact you.

On the other hand, if you are writing an op-ed column, feel free to spray whatever's in your heart without the slightest bit of research. No one can fact-check an opinion. Make sure you refer to anyone you disagree with as a 'snowflake'. They think they're precious and unique but they are actually fragile, and it's not a reference to the colour of their skin, as you accuse them of fraudulently taking government funding and benefits as an Indigenous Australian.

Celebrated investigative journalist Kate McClymont famously brought down corrupt NSW politician Eddie Obeid by looking up his Wikipedia entry and copying and pasting it.

What other sides to a story are there, other than the true one?

Before you finish your article, it's important to have all the facts at your disposal. This doesn't mean, however, 'things that actually happened' is your only source of information. Ask around Google the topic of your piece and see what dissenting opinions pop up. Remember, quotes are great for filling out a word count, and as long as you link back to the original source,

"Tired? Stressed?"

So was Radek Sali. And then he found a way to get people to pay $60 for a bottle of tablets that don't work. Then he sold the company, and now tours the world with models and movie stars. So no, it's not stressful at all.

Swisse ***"You'll feel better when you own Swisse!"***

Hold power to account
One advantage of becoming a journalist is that you become a member of a proud profession that seeks to hold power to account, one listicle at a time.

What is a sub?

PEDANTS **Sub-editors.** They were an important part of the journalistic process but since all that stuff got outsourced to the call-centre equivalent of fact-checkers and Microsoft Word's spellcheck function, they now gather in Facebook groups like 'Horny handed subs of toil' to grouse about typos and to ask why writers never learn that it's 'just deserts' not 'just desserts' and ask when it became acceptable to say 'obligated' when you mean 'obliged'. Mamas, don't let your babies grow up to be grammar Nazis. They won't get a job.

you're good to grab as much direct speech as possible. After all, if someone says something in public, that makes it public domain.

Anyway, you should be treating every story as though it was a journalistic Rashômon. If it's about coral bleaching in the Great Barrier Reef, grab a quote from an Adani spokesperson, a local surfer, Tony Abbott and the owner of a scuba diving company (doesn't have to be a Queenslander, obviously). That way, you'll have plenty of words to put on the page, without having to pass judgement on anyone's opinion. That's for the reader to decide.

And, well, the subs who fact-check the piece, write the captions and headline. Hahaha-hahahaha...

Washington Post investigative journalists Bob Woodward and Carl Bernstein famously brought down the Nixon Administration through the dissemination of FAKE NEWS.

The golden rule of journalism

ALAN RAMSAY The golden rule of journalism is that things were way better before you got here, you pissant little rookie. Now get the fuck out of here with that recording app. Can't you read shorthand? Your round, pipsqueak.

PETE EVANS' BACK TO BASICS TIPS

"I got my teeth professionally whitened, just like the cavemen"

COOK UP YOUR OWN CONSPIRACY THEORIES

Pre-packaged conspiracy theories can be overly processed and full of nasties. Much better to whip up your own ideas using home-grown facts. The best bit is, you always know where the ingredients came from - your imagination!

GET YOUR TEETH PROFESSIONALLY WHITENED

Nothing says back-to-basics like an expensive cosmetic dental procedure custom-made for television. Get the sparkling smile which made our cave-dwelling ancestors famous, with a professional teeth whitening. It's quick, easy, and screams 'au naturel'.

LOWER YOUR FACT INTAKE

High-fact debates might seem appetising, but they're terrible for book sales. Since taking facts right out of my diet I've never felt better.

CREATE YOUR OWN HEALTH ADVICE

And turn it into a feature-length Netflix documentary. Telling people that eating carbohydrates can lead to autism or cancer was a totally liberating experience for me.

AVOID NASTIES LIKE SUNCREAM

I prefer the warm glow of an all-natural skin cancer. You should be very sceptical of Big Suncream - why would you trust an organisation that stops young children dying?

APPLY THE WORD 'TOXIN' LIBERALLY

I spread it through most of my books and articles. It gives the impression that something is bad, without having to go through the hassle of explaining why! Make sure you have a book, product, or expensive diet program for sale that magically eradicates the toxin - then watch the dollars flow in!

Good sources of information, versus elitist ones

If you want to be known as a brilliant writer who leaves a gasping, select audience of hand-picked readers in awe with every dripping jewel of crafted prose, go write an allegorical novel about a clumsy vixen's sexual awakening at the hands of a smooth-handed scribe, or become a columnist for *The Monthly*. Most normal readers don't give a shit about your throwaway references to fin de siècle political movements or Kurosawa films or what Ben Chifley would have thought about all of this. That goes double for your sources. Don't be a goddamn elitist. No one likes it, and no one clicks on it. Here's a handy guide to sourcing your material.

YOUR UNCLE AFTER FOUR WOODSTOCKS: GOOD
A FEDERAL POLITICIAN: BAD

Ask yourself this: who's going to be better informed about what's going wrong with this once-great nation? Your uncle, who spends all day trawling through a huge variety of Facebook groups dedicated to the pure love of Australia, or some bastard politician who's robbing pensioners to pay queue-jumpers to take jobs from disabled battlers who shouldn't be on welfare in the first place if they're able to join a protest march against our brave boys fighting ISIS so that every child of the Southern Cross can continue to celebrate Australia Day on January 26 as God and Captain Arthur Phillip intended, no matter what this smart-arsed Andrew P Street bloke your cousin keeps sharing on my bloody wall just to stir me up – and it's not bloody working mate, trust me – might have to say about it? Fair dinkum, more dollars than sense, some people.

MAN IN THE STREET: GOOD
ANDREW P STREET: BAD

There's a reason that we talk about political ideas passing the pub test. It's because the man in the street is a very good judge of what's bullshit. Fairfax columnist Andrew P Street, on the other hand, is an Adelaide-born elitist who only pretends to like Barnesy and sneers at your greatest hits albums. Don't quote him. Unless he's standing in the street. Or a pub, I suppose. Actually, this is a grey area.

TWITTER: GOOD
PEER-REVIEWED JOURNAL: BAD

Everyone's on Twitter these days. It's relatable. Plus it's heaps easier to search than the university library.

A CLOSE FRIEND OF THE COUPLE: GOOD
THE PERSON WHO ACTUALLY SAID IT: BAD

This one's specific to gossip mags, mostly. You might think it's more hoity-toity to throw around anonymous sources, like you're Woodward and Bernstein grabbing confidential information from Deep Throat or whatever (I never got to the end of that film), but really, it's way more elitist to name-check the people who are so close to a celebrity couple on the rocks that they know the intimate details of their trainwreck relationship, but not so close that they wouldn't anonymously sell out said couple in the glossy pages of some scandalous publication. As an unrelated serendipitous bonus, it's heaps harder for Bec and Lleyton to sue if they don't know who said all that shit about them.

WIKIPEDIA: GOOD
ANYTHING ELSE: BAD

If the boss is riding you, I suppose it's okay to click on one of those footnotes to see where the info originally came from, but seriously, Wikipedia's laden down with editors who are hyperfocused on ensuring the correct information is present and correct in each entry. Plus, it's all free so you don't even have to say 'according to Wikipedia' when you're presenting the facts of the matter. It's a given that it's from Wikipedia.

The Shovel's Guide to

NATUROPATHS

Is your blood flowing incorrectly? Do you worry that the foods you eat could contain *chemicals*? Does your regular doctor have no idea about how urine facials or electromagnetic cleansing work?

If you answered yes to any of these questions, you need a naturopath!

Here's how to find the right alternative to medicine for you...

PRIORITISE THE POWER OF POSITIVE THINKING

The number one cause of incurable diseases is negativity. So choose a naturopath who has unwavering faith in their healing skills. Then, once you truly believe that your naturopath's diet and lifestyle advice will stimulate your body's innate healing abilities, you'll be well on your way to thinking you're cured.

LOOK FOR A GOOD LISTENER

Listening without exercising any judgement is a naturopath's greatest skill. Find someone who will sit and listen for hours* as you explain how filtering your previously fluoridated shower water has radically improved your ability to tolerate gluten, dairy, meat, vegetables, seafood, eggs, small children, and loud noises. You'll feel better afterwards.

RE-EXAMINE YOUR DEFINITION OF "GOOD"

Think about what you really want from your health practitioner.

For some, a good naturopath will find remedies that fit with their current lifestyle choices. For others, the measure of a naturopath is how many followers they have on YouTube.

CHECK FOR INSTANT-DIAGNOSIS EQUIPMENT

One of the best things about naturopaths is that they can perform most of their tests on-the-spot. Look for a naturopath who has a complete functional medicine toolkit, including:

HIMALAYAN SALT LAMP

This is a great, non-intrusive tool for assessing your ability to detect warm light.

TINCTURES

Ingesting a small, potentially lethal dose of an unknown substance is a highly effective way to immediately put your liver and kidney function to the test.

SACRED GEOMETRY FLASHCARDS

With this one quick quiz, your naturopath can evaluate multiple areas of your cognitive function, including scientific awareness and response to the power of suggestion.

*billable

essence of
PLACEBOLIUM

Exciting destinations!
Horrible service!

World's worst airline!*

Jetstuffed

* Ranked 73rd out of 73 International Airline Survey 2017

Tips for traditional journalists

How to misrepresent major news stories

By Rupert Murdoch

Despite what some people claim, the news isn't just about 'facts' and 'reporting the truth', there's a whole lot more nuance when it comes to being a journalist, from chasing up leads, to double-checking sources, to selling out your core values to a billionaire who uses his media outlets as a political tool because you have a family to feed and he's the only one employing journalists these days.

Global Warming

BAD: This young child was forced to take a year off school to beg the world's 6 billion adults for some leadership to stop a mass extinction event

GOOD: Girl throws tantrum at UN

Migrant exodus

BAD: 40 consecutive years of western destabilisation has forced people in the Middle East to flee their homes

GOOD: **Asylum seekers are stealing jobs**

Fires destroying the east coast

BAD: Fires are getting worse due to climate change despite arson rates dropping

GOOD: **200 fires lit by arsonists this year**

Transgender people

BAD: 99 in 100 doctors say hormone blockers are safest treatment for trans teenagers

GOOD: **One doctor claims PC parents are forcing children to take gender changing drugs**

How to know if you're food intolerance intolerant

Do you have trouble stomaching the idea that some people can't eat certain things?
Do the veins in your forehead bulge whenever somebody orders a soy latte?
Does the sight of a gluten free label cause you to wheeze uncontrollably?
If so, you may be suffering from a food intolerance intolerance. Here's how to deal with it.

Step 1.
Be sure to always loudly complain about how much vegans always loudly complain, whenever you see a vegan option on a menu.

Step 2.
Don't just take people's word for it. Always try to test the idea that certain foods might make people's airways close up by subtly sneaking it into their meals just to prove a point.

Step 3.
Learn to mind your own fucking business.

This is the only known cure for food intolerance intolerances, and fortunately it has a 100% success rate.

Before you know it you'll be back to being able to eat whatever the fuck you want, just like you have always been free to do.

1/2 PRICE OFF RRP^

^50% OFF RRP EXCLUDES THE BLACKMORES SUPERFOODS RANGE

Swisse®

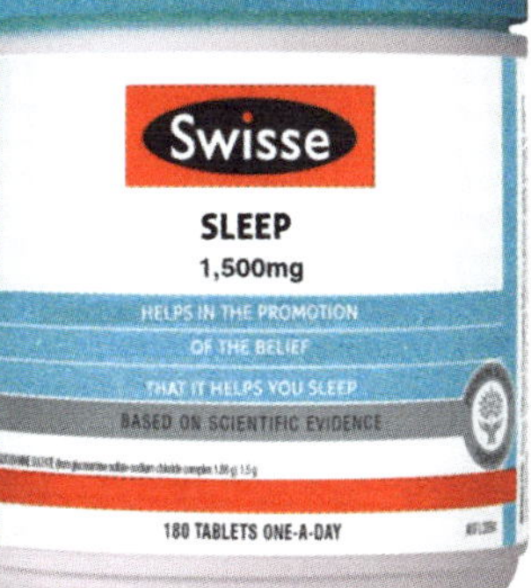

$33.29

$18.39

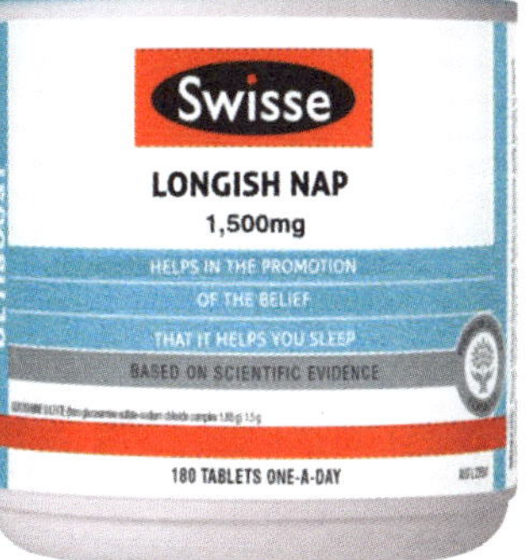

$32.49

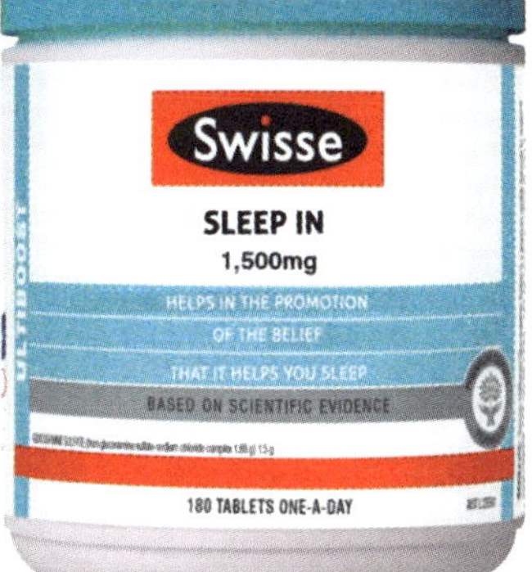

$26.99

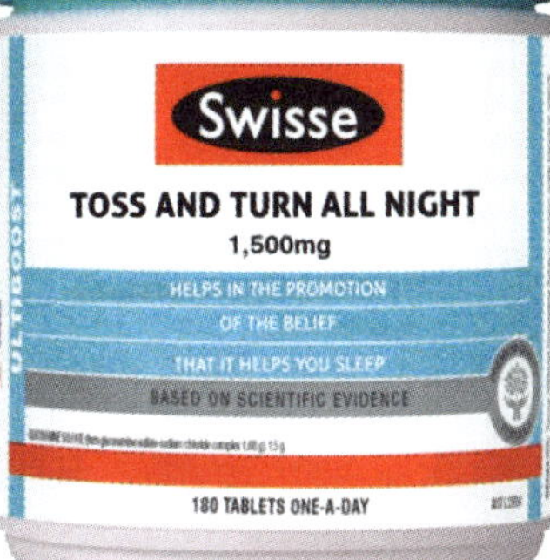

$33.29

$45.39

$31.79

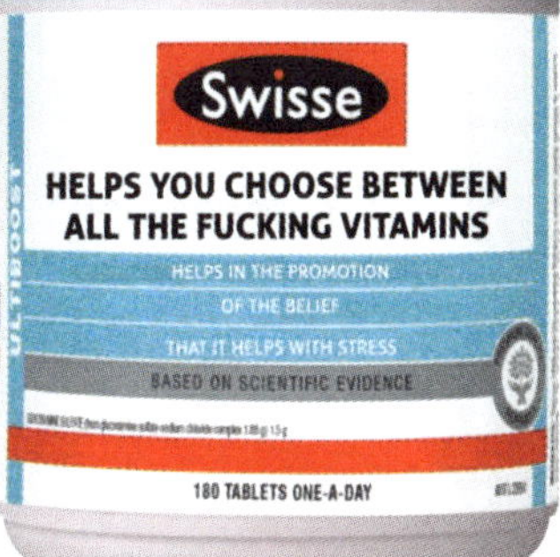

$18.99

$21.24

$26.49

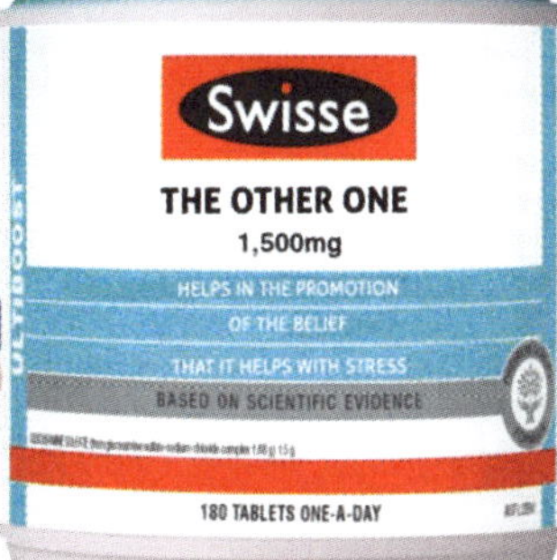

$32.49

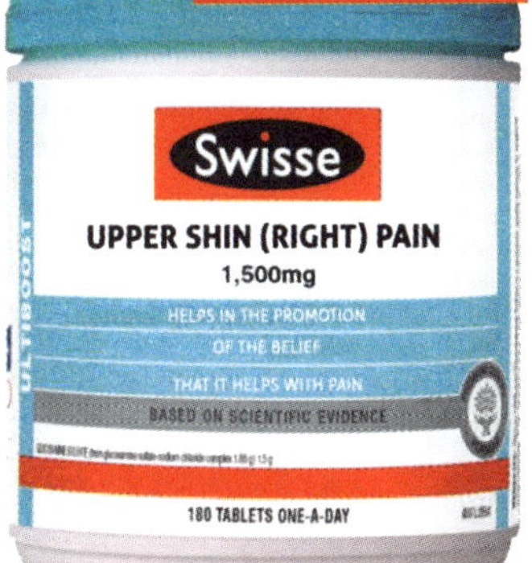

$25.99

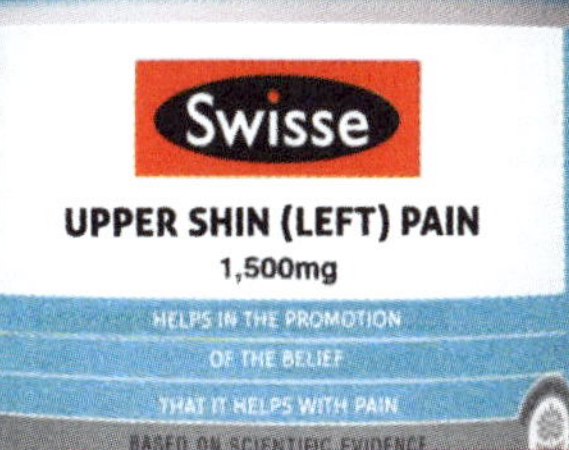

$39.99

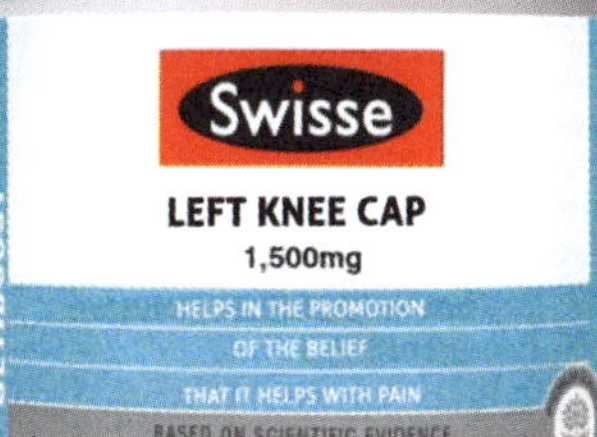

$78.79

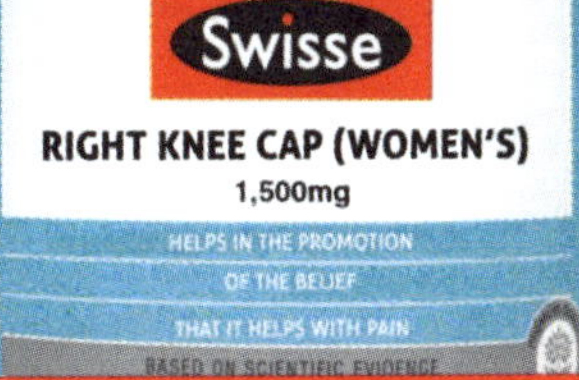

Stop Paying Too Much!!

CHEMIST WAREHOUSE

DISCOUNT CHEMIST

WWW.CHEMISTWAREHOUSE.COM.AU

Bushfires and Arson

There's been a lot of chatter in the past few months about whether the terrible bushfires that swept across much of Australia over summer were caused by arson or climate change.

This is a good question, and not a stupid question that "conflates ignition-type with fuel-source" as some "experts" would have you believe.

But whether you're a died-in-the-wool greenie or an ordinary everyday climate skeptic who doesn't believe every statement that's printed on the back of your kombucha bottle, I always say: when you're worried about something because an expert has told it to you, there's only one thing to do: do your own research.

Data or cause?

'Scientists' claim Austria's largest glacier, the Pasterze, is shrinking rapidly. But the signposts which mark the retreating position of ice each year, may in fact be scaring away the ice, causing the problem.

THE EXPERIMENT

The question that we need to resolve is this: "Are bushfires caused by arson or climate change?"

Climate loonies claim that bushfires are burning longer and more intensely than thirty years ago. But is that actually true?

To answer this question, I decided to light a bushfire and see whether it burned longer and more intensely than the bushfire I lit 30 years ago.

I decided to light the fire in the exact same piece of virgin bushland as I did thirty years ago, to make sure the results were as comparable as possible, and to eliminate as many variables as possible.

CHALLENGES

When you're doing your own research, you often come up against people who tell you not to. That's a typical response by experts, who don't want their own privileged position on the knowledge tree threatened by amateurs like me.

This time round, even the police told me I shouldn't do my own research! The police are supposed to be an impartial bunch, but instead even they have been captured by the environmental lobby.

THE EXPERIMENT

I can definitively confirm that the bushfire I lit this year burned longer and more intensely than the one I lit thirty years ago.

While this may appear to be a slam dunk for climate change activists, I can 100% confirm that the fire was definitely started through arson, which kind of muddies the waters somewhat. Clearly more research is needed.

Unfortunately, my lawyer says, I can't say much more than that about that particular fire at this stage as it is the subject of several civil lawsuits, as well as criminal proceedings. Such is the life of an iconoclast.

REPLICABILITY?

Clearly one bushfire doesn't prove anything.

Some people criticised me for not conducting the experiment in a way that is easy replicable. But to that I say: YES I DID.

I'm proud to say that during the summer, I repeated my experiment a total of 183 times.

RESULTS

For every single one of the 183 bushfires I studied, the bushfire appeared to burn longer and more intensely than in previous years, but – and here's the shocking truth – every single one of the 183 fires I lit was caused by arson.

CONCLUSION

Why are bushfires burning longer and more intensely?

One obvious conclusion is that arsonists are getting better. Thirty years ago I was a hapless 14 year old boy with a court-mandated order against purchasing lighters, matches and other sources of ignition. Now I have no restrictions whatsoever, and have degree in fire dynamics.

Another conclusion is that the climate is, indeed, leading to drier, hotter conditions. I think it's fair to say it's too early to tell whether this is true, and more study is required. Perhaps in another thirty years we'll have our answer. Who knows?

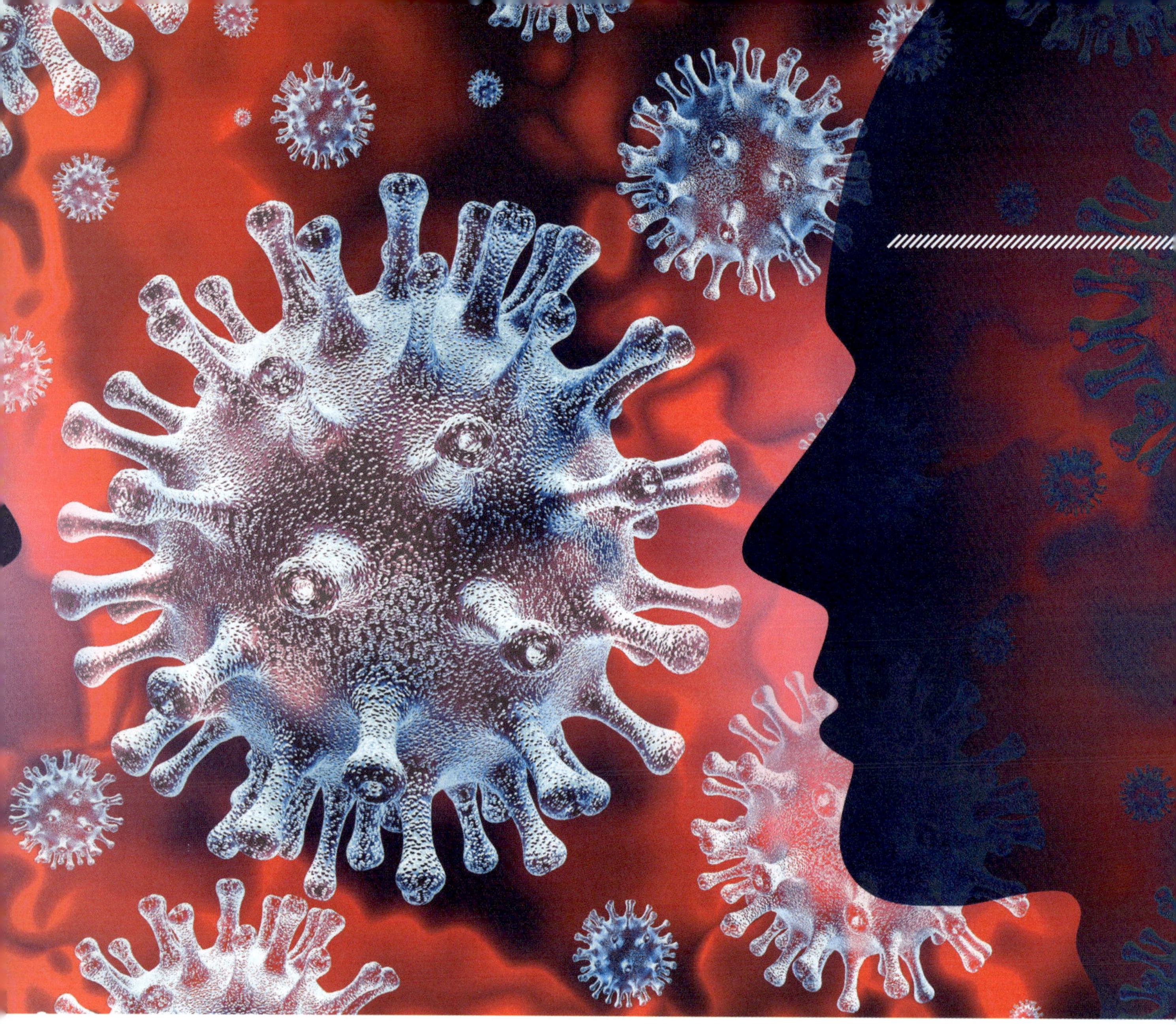

How to Protect yourself from the Coronavirus the Natural Way

If you're one of the smart ones who does just take expert's advice at face value, then you've probably realised that the COVID-19 Coronavirus is fake, dreamed up by the Centre for Disease Control, in concert with the CIA and the Chinese Communist Party in order to line the pockets of Big Pharma. However, in the unlikely event that it is real, here are some tips about how to protect yourself that you won't hear from the "experts" who "know what they're talking about".

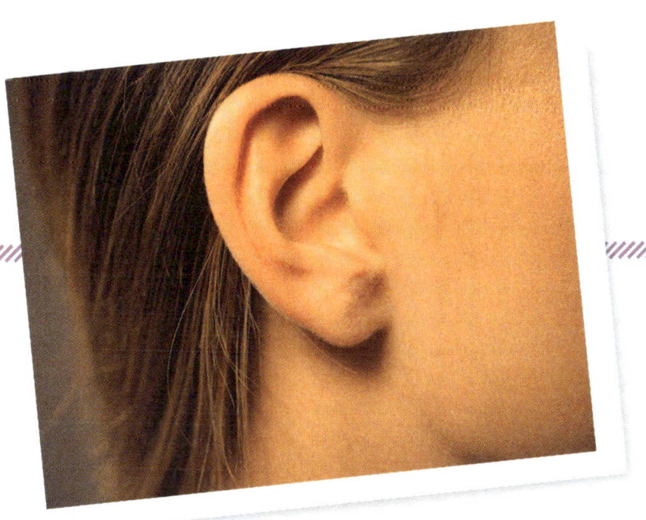

ABOVE:
In a double blind test, 100% of people who didn't put a candle in their ear were found to be completely Corona virus free.

RIGHT: These facemasks do nothing, the man is dead now.

1. Put a candle in your ear

According to Medical News Daily, "Ear candling is an unsafe and unproven practice during which a person inserts a lit candle into their ear. The heat from the candle is supposed to draw earwax and other impurities out of the ear."

Sounds pretty bad, huh? But that just proves it works. If a respected medical newsletter says it's unproven, obviously they're opposing it for a reason. That reason could be that it works so well that it will put the entire medical profession out of a job. They're just trying to stop you curing yourself so that they can line their own pockets by curing you.

While nobody has tried ear candling on the coronavirus, it makes sense that it should work, since a virus is an "impurity" that needs to be drawn out of your body, ideally through the ear.

2. Don't put a candle in your ear

This is somewhat anecdotal, and it may seem to be at odds with the previous tip, but having talked to several people who don't put candles in their ears, NONE of them have the coronavirus, which suggests that not putting a candle in your ear is a cheap and effective prophylactic against the virus. In fact, in my informal study, the correlation between not having a candle in your ear and not having coronavirus is 100%. Obviously further research is needed, and it's still unclear why not putting a candle in your ear might have this effect, but some have suggested that perhaps coronaviruses are transmitted by sticking onto the end of candles, and by not putting one in your ear, it cuts down the risk of exposure through this method. Fascinating!

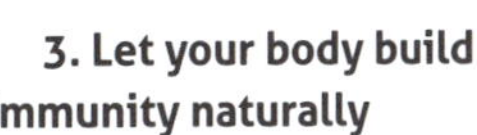

3. Let your body build immunity naturally

Obviously you can't trust vaccinations because they're a government conspiracy, but you can achieve roughly the same result by getting your hands on a small sample of the coronavirus and then building a ISO 15189:2012 Medical laboratory. Once you've done that, go into the virus's RNA and deactivate the parts that cause harm in humans, and then grow the virus in a culture or egg, and then use a syringe to inject a small amount of that deactivated virus into your body.

Your body's immune system will promptly start creating anti-bodies against the virus, and within a few days, your immune system will be trained to fight off the coronavirus should it come your way. Easy! And natural!

Did you know? Coronavirus can be neutralised by alcohol. While this may sound like good news to all Australians, unfortunately the level of alcohol that would be required in your bloodstream to kill the virus is over 70% alcohol to blood ratio, which could kill you, or worse - you could be promoted to leader of the National Party.

Don't quit quitting!
One of the best things about a Breatharian diet is that it cuts through many of the false debates in the dieting community. For example, with Breatharianism, it's not a matter of whether or not you should skip breakfast or not. Breakfast doesn't even exist!

4. Eat only organic fruits and uncooked root vegetables

If you adopt a diet entirely consisting of organic fruit and uncooked root vegetables, after a few days you'll be so sick of your diet, you'll wish you had the coronavirus.

While this, strictly speaking, won't protect you from the coronavirus, if you happen to get it, it'll be something that you'd wished for. What a flip!

What's more, by switching to an all-vegetable diet, it will also have the added advantage of lowering your climate emissions considerably - the only downside being that it will be balanced out by the emissions of you having to tell everyone you've gone vegan, and all the hack standup comedy that will produce.

Eating large amounts of broccoli is believed to improve the quality of telomeres, which could be the key to immortality in humans, if only the all-broccoli diet didn't make people want to kill themselves.

5. Eat nothing but meat

Once again, the all meat diet - popularised by controversial life guru Jordan Peterson - won't cure Coronavirus per se. However, based on Peterson's results there is a good chance this so called 'anti-inflammatory prehistoric diet' it will see you wind up in a Russian Private Hospital recovering from a tranquilliser addiction, and frankly we couldn't think of a better place to hide out while you wait for a viral pandemic to blow over.

6. Buy Vitamins from ChaserShop.com

The Chaser sells a range of multivitamins and other scientifically unproven remedies against coronavirus on its website ChaserShop.com.

Check out our Discount Warehouse style pricing, where everything is always 60% off its listed price.

Can I personally recommend our special "Gullibility Guard" formulation. These pills can help protect you from gullibly falling for natural remedies that don't work.

Simply take forty pills per day, and if you begin to suspect the treatment is itself a scam,

The P2 Facemask - Does it work?

Many people have written to us asking whether the P2 facemask actually works to prevent the coronavirus.

To answer your question, our first instinct was to turn to Google, but we all know how unreliable health advice from Google can be, don't we!

So instead, we turned to one of the most educated people on the topic we could find - a mother on a Facebook comment section who has 'done her research'.

According to Kathy, these P2 facemasks are ugly, and she won't be caught dead wearing one.

So there you have it! If you have any other health questions, probably don't mail us because these magazines are very intermittent and you'll probably be dead before you get a reply.

it means it's WORKING and you should not stop taking them.

But hurry before we're shut down under the Trade Practices Act for Deceptive and Misleading practices. Typical nanny state!

Disclaimer: The Chaser Quarterly is in no way affiliated with ChaserShop.com.

Any similarity in the name, logo, board members, or people making the profits off of this advertorial, is purely coincidental.

Swisse Choose Between All the Fucking Vitamins with FREE Gullibility Guard

$35.99 ~~$89.99~~

Add to cart

FREE BOTTLE OF GULLIBILITY GUARD WITH EVERY PURCHASE

Do you find yourself endlessly confused by the number of vitamins you need to buy just to function in modern life. You need Swisse "Helps You Choose Between All the Fucking Vitamins".

It's scientific formula will leave you and your wallet feeling lighter than ever before.

Swisse Choose Between All the Fucking Vitamins helps in the natural formation of superprofits for the owners of Swisse.

Buy now and for a limited time, we'll throw in a free bottle of Gullibility Guard with every purchase.

Help I'm trapped in a captioning factory 

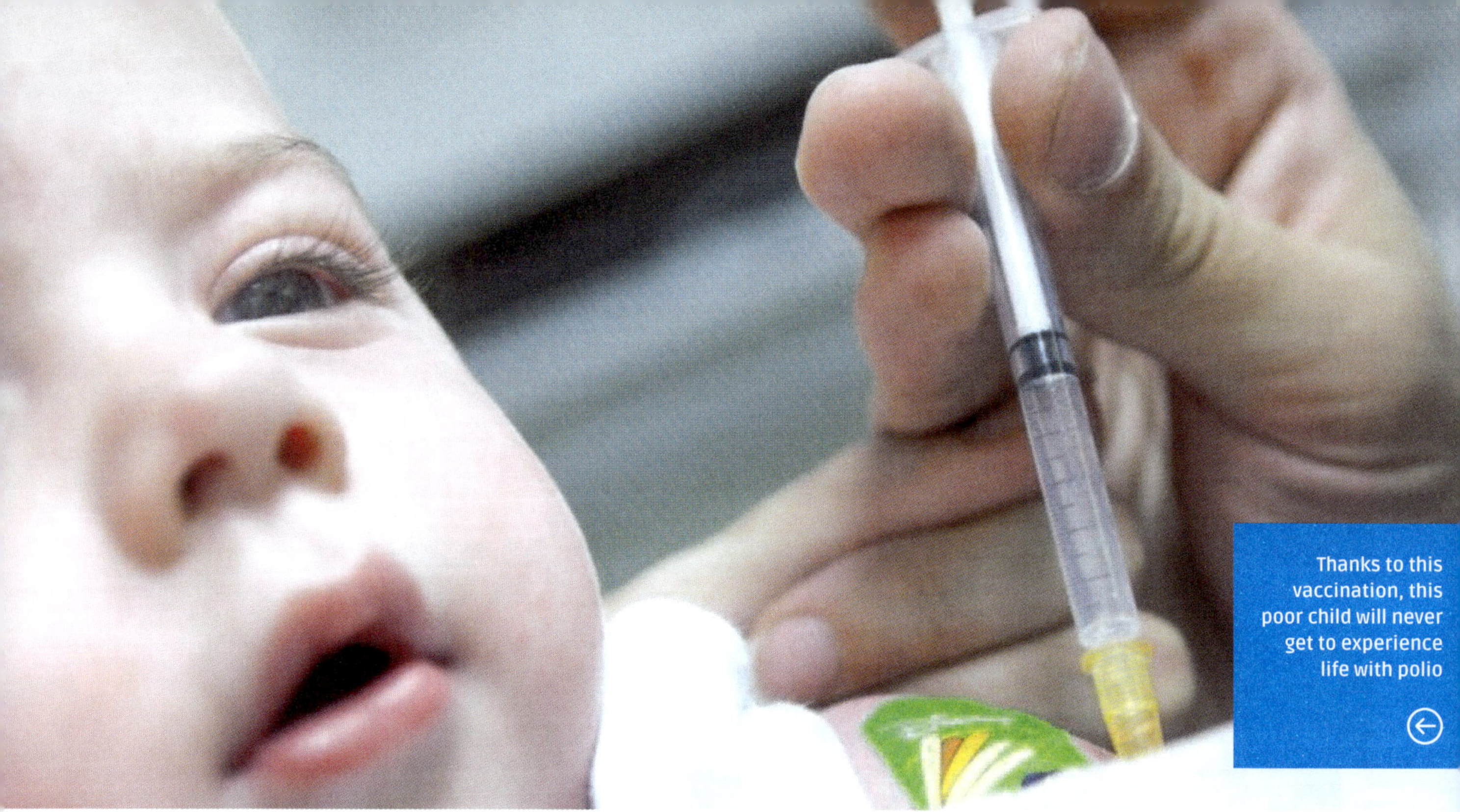

Thanks to this vaccination, this poor child will never get to experience life with polio

Forced to get your child vaccinated? Try this one simple trick to avoid autism

As a mother, I'm aware many parents these days have valid concerns about the effects vaccines may be having on their children. However, with recent government crackdowns on parents who choose to not immunise their children, it can be difficult to avoid.

However, very few parents know that there is a simple trick that can be employed so that your child is marked as vaccinated on medical registers, without putting them at risk of any chemicals that may be present. In fact, I've done this on my own children to great results.

The process is simple. Set up a regular vaccination schedule with your local GP, making sure you book only morning appointments if possible (this is when your child's body will still be more hydrated, increasing the saline content in their blood thanks to their natural sleep induced retention). Make sure you visit with the child when the injections are received, and do not alert the doctor to the fact that you are employing a vaccine reduction programme (they may alert health authorities).

Now, the important part, and you'll be surprised how simple it is. After your child has received the vaccination shot (and you are safely away from the clinic) press a cut onion to your child's skin at the point of puncture. Onions are a rare vegetable in that they are made up of thousands of fluid filled capillaries, which when cut drop in pressure. By applying the onion with some light pressure to the skin within 5 minutes of the vaccine being injected, they will begin to draw it back out of your child's arm through a process known as 'capillary action' the same way trees draw liquid from the soil in order to live. The natural pressure in your child's body means that the injected vaccine fluid is already under pressure and will easily leak out, the onion not only draws this fluid from the tissue of the body, but its acidity also prevents the puncture wound from healing while still applied to the skin, ensuring that almost none of the vaccine is left after 10 minutes of application.

So there it is, it's that simple. According to your child's doctors, schools, daycare, and medical records they are completely vaccinated, but you can rest easy in the peace of mind that no toxins are putting your child's health at risk.

Pete Evans's Top Four Fads for 2020

Diet anti-expert Pete Evans shares all the latest fads that your previously sane friends will get swept up in this year, along with the perfect vitamin deficiencies to pair them with.

Skipping every meal

INSPIRING

Did you know 100% of people who skip every meal never get cancer? Forget last year's fads of skipping breakfast, or intermittent fasting - the new 'eat absolutely nothing' diet is going to be all the rage in 2020 especially among interns.

Not Drinking

MASCULINE

Chris Hemsworth recently revealed that in order to appear muscular on-screen, Hollywood hunks must go without liquids for 72 hours to avoid appearing 'bloated'. So that's the new normal guys, get on it.

Battery Acid Vinegar

DARING

2019 was the year of Apple Cider Vinegar, with many celebrities gushing about the benefits of a daily glass of the highly corrosive acid to help with weight loss. In 2020, why not go one step futher and just completely dissolve your insides with a fresh glass of battery acid? Yum!

Anus Uranium

THE MARIE CUREALL

Step aside Gwenyth Paltrow, jade eggs in your vagina is so last year. Inspired the revolutionary full body skinpeel from the smash hit TV show Chernobyl, this year is all about the healthy green glow that can only be attained by shelving some imported Russian yellowcake.

> The President, Vice-President, and all civil officers of the United States, shall be removed from office on impeachment for, and conviction of, treason, bribery, or other high crimes and misdemeanors.
>
> - Article II, Section 4 of the now-defunct US Consitution

TEXT Charles Firth   **PHOTO** Getty Images

The Anti-Expert's Guide to American Democracy

Until 2017, the United States was overrun with experts. All elected officials were answerable to a set of rules drafted by LOSERS. As you can imagine, that was a hopeless way to run everything. Nowadays things are much better because there are no experts in sight of the Oval Office. Here is how the system works.

AMERICAN DEMOCRACY was a process, whereby, every four years, the national political system entered a deadlock for two years to select two people to run against each other, each of whom represented different segments of the business community.

Then every citizen in the nation got the chance to vote on who they wanted, after which the majority opinion was disregarded. The role was then given to whoever was better at Twitter.

The President was then expected to spend the next four years selling-out his biggest supporters to the business community.

The founding fathers were the patriarchial products of the late 18th century, and did not grant women the right to vote. Likewise, Donald Trump is a patriarchial product of the late 18th century.

US LEGAL SYSTEM HIERARCHY

BEFORE 2001:

National Rifle Association

The Constitution

Supreme Court

Laws of Congress

Presidential Decrees

AFTER 2001:

Airport Security

The Patriot Act

Supreme Court

Foreign Press Correspondents' Dinner speeches

The Constitution

AFTER 2017:

Donald Trump's Twitter feed

Laws of Congress that @RealDonaldTrump retweets

The Constitution's 2nd Amendment

The Constitution (of Russia)

The Constitution

Until 2017, the Constitution of the United States was a set of guidelines describing how the United States would function if it didn't have a Supreme Court. Nowadays it is an interesting, if esoteric, piece of memorabilia.

Until 2001, the Constitution was considered a binding document, and laws were invalid if they violated the principals set out in the Constitution. Then after the 9/11 attacks, the Constitution was converted into an 'advisory only' document. The only remaining binding clause in it was the second amendment, which allowed Americans the right to shoot unarmed black people at night.

The Patriot Act became the the highest law of the land.

Cut out this quick reference guide to the US Legal System, for easy reference in case you become the next target of the regime.

Many clauses in the constitution were ruled invalid for violating the lack of principals outlined in the Patriot Act.

The Supreme Court

Until 2017, it was the Supreme Court's function to interpret the Constitution. Back then, there were two bodies of thought about how the Constitution should be interpreted. Conservatives believed that the Constitution should be interpreted as literally as possible except when they disagreed with it.

A crazed despotic tyrant with daddy issues meets with Kim Jong Un

Trump with Kim Jong Un: Shealah Craighead/Official White House Photo, Oval Office signing law: Ron Sachs

Concerned about the state of American politics? There are plenty of online petitions to make you feel better. Go online and sign some today. Or better yet, don't. It's just as effective!

Liberals, on the other hand, believed the Constitution was a living, breathing document that should have been interpreted as broadly as possible, as long as there was a majority of liberals on the bench.

For example, conservatives believed that the 'right to bear arms' gave them the inalienable right to run a scare campaign about Big Government taking away your guns after each major massacre in order to fundraise for the National Rifle Association.

On the other hand, liberals believed that the 'right to bear arms' didn't even give you the right to bring a semi-automatic machine gun to church without filling out a whole lot of forms.

Until 2017, the US Constitution was notoriously hard to change. It required agreement from two-thirds of states, plus a vote in both houses of Congress. This meant that only uncontroversial things, such as the criminalisation of alcohol had traditionally been able to be ratified.

Over the years, politicians found that it was easier to ignore the Constitution, and then appoint judges willing to look the other way.

Nowadays the Constitution is interpreted in two ways. In the first instance, the meaning of laws or orders are clarified through the @realDonaldTrump twitter account. If a deeper, more extensive interpretation is required, or if Donald Trump is playing golf, the constitutional law is interpreted through an op-ed on Breibart.com. If there is still debate, the constitutionality of a law is ultimately determined by how many retweets the idea gets on Donald Trump's feed.

The Parties

Until 2017, there were two major parties in US politics. The Democratic Party was the party of people who are naively optimistic about how the US political system works. These are comprised of a coalition of interests who have only achieved broad-based political rights in the last few decades, people such as women, Latinos, Blacks, LGBTQI and other ethnic communities. They were in coalition with the college educated and union workers. The Republicans were a less inclusive church, comprising mainly of people who fall for spam emails.

As you can imagine, the Democratic Party won the popular vote in a landslide, by almost three million votes. Even so, the Republican Party still controls the Senate in Congress and the Executive Branch. And this result came about apparently while the system was still 'working'.

The future of the Democratic Party remains in the balance. Some diehard supporters still believe that winning at the ballot box later this year will deliver them power. So at least they haven't lost their sense of humour. ★

Before an executive order can be used to breach the Constitution, it must be signed by the President

FREE SCRATCH AND SNIFF CORONAVIRUS SAMPLE

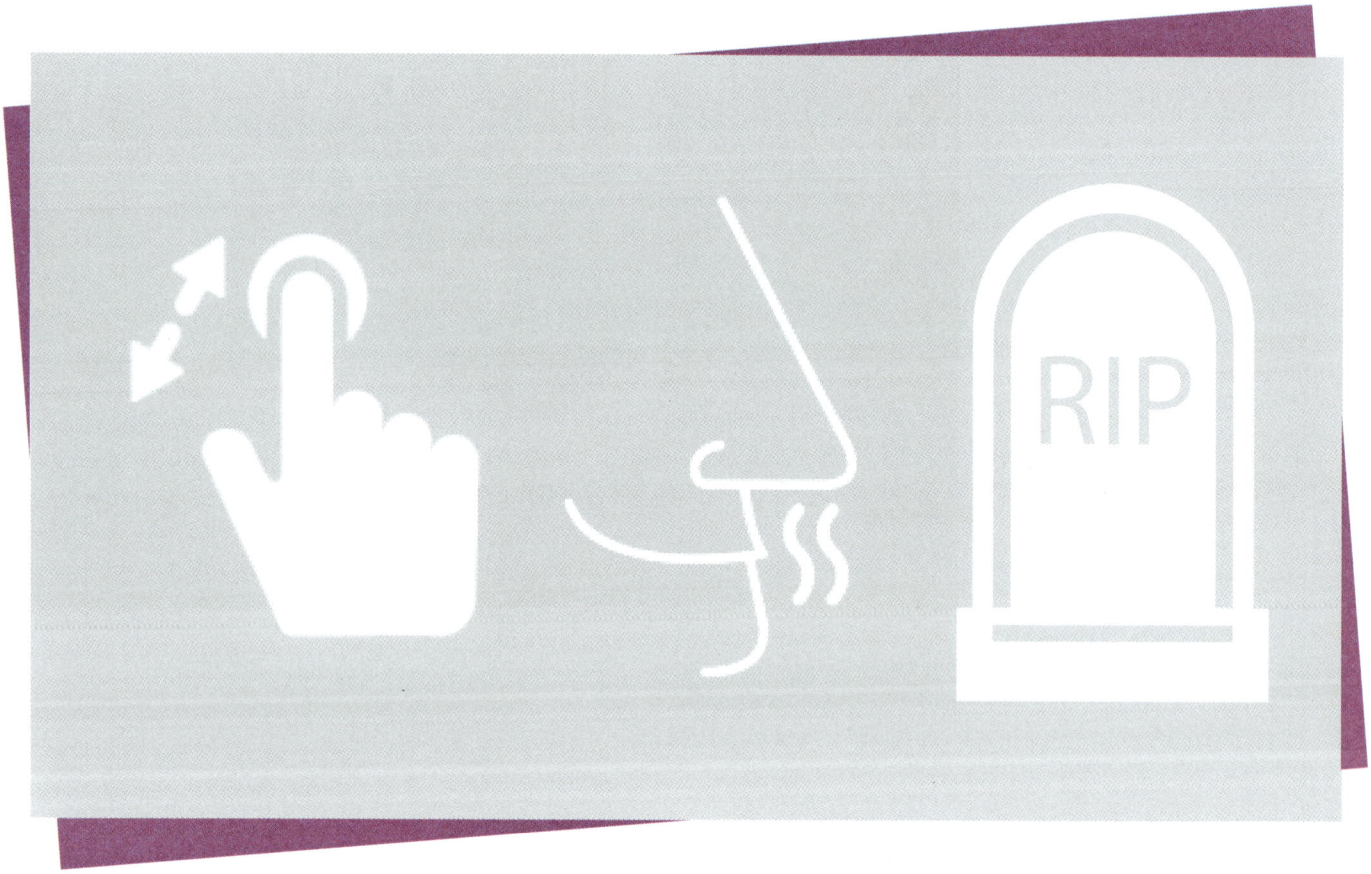
RIP

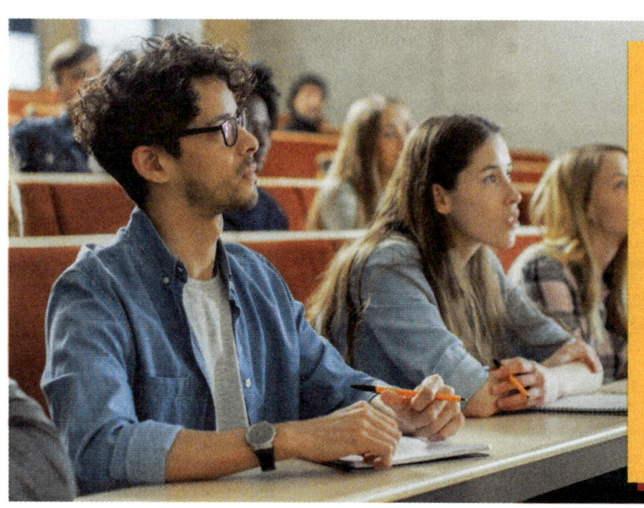

EDUCATE YOURSELF
Do you want an education that doesn't revolve around lecture halls and textbooks?
Do you have a car as your profile picture?
Do you want to weigh in on complex topics despite have absolutely no understanding or experience in the field?
The University of Life is now open for enrolments from literally anyone on Facebook with an uninformed opinion on climate change.
UNIVERSITY OF LIFE
Who needs qualifications
To apply to the university of life, simply visit Facebook.com and leave an angry comment about the ABC

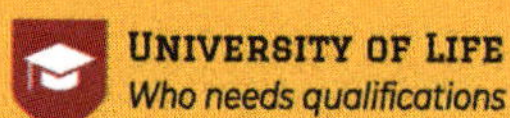

Dear customers,

We know some of you have been worried recently about the alleged links between Corona Beer and the Corona Virus. So, to put your minds at ease, we're releasing a new, re-branded Corona beer.

It's the same great taste, with a much more reassuring name. We hope you like it as much as we enjoyed making it.

The Anti-Expert's Guide to THE ZODIAC

Do you ever read your star sign and think: "this feels like it's just made up"? Too often horoscopes are written by people who know very little about the Zodiac.

Experts might tell you it's "unscientific" and "has no evidence to support any of its claims", but that's probably because they're a Capricorn and they're just being stubborn.

We decided to get someone who knows all about the Zodiac to write , and who better to get than the ZODIAC KILLER himself.

TAURUS April 22 - May 21

Look at you sitting there. You're slouching again. Think of your back, shouldn't you be looking after it more, do you want to be like your parents at their age? Yes, that's right correct your posture.

You're enjoying this brief moment of down time aren't you, just one look at your face tells me that. I mean, don't get me wrong, you and me both know you like being social, but sometimes you find it nice to just unwind and read something, off in your own world, where nobody is going to judge you wearing that outfit, even though you've worn it a thousand times before.

How's your knee by the way? I know it caused problems in the past. Do you think it's because of the accident you had as a child that caused the small scar on your leg? Yes that one. You can't remember the details of what happened can you. But I can. I've been watching you for years. Even through those rough teenage years when you thought you were alone. Don't believe me? That's what I knew you'd say. I know you don't like people telling you what you think do you? You've always naturally questioned things. That's what I like about you. That and your hair, even if you're self conscious about it. What's that noise on the window, you wonder? Probably a branch. Don't look.

Favourite colours: Pale White, Blood Red
Favourite phrases: "Hello? Is anyone there?" and "No! Don't kill me!"
Celebrity killers who share your star sign: H.H. Holmes, Michael Ryan, Albert Fish, David Copeland, Levi Bellfield, Robert Black, Steve Wright, Orville Lynn Majors

GEMINI May 22 - June 20

As a Gemini, you like games. What a coincidence! So do I. Let's play one. It's called: Guess Who's Hiding in Your Closet With A Large Knife and A Reel of Gaffer Tape?

Give up? It was me! I'm disappointed you gave up so easily. I thought Geminis were more dynamic than that. Geminis are supposed to have many talents. But your only talent seems to be staring back in terror with your mouth wide open.

Favourite numbers: 9, 1 and 1.
Favourite phrase: "This isn't funny Mark, stop messing around! Mark?"
Celebrity killers who share your star sign: Jeffrey Dahmer, David Berkowitz, Ted Kaczynski

CANCER June 21-July 22

You're sensitive and friend-oriented, which makes you the easiest mark I've ever met. Wanna hang out? Let's go to this great bar I know. It's just down this laneway. Yep, I'm sure it's this way.

You have a practical side which allows you to take calculated risks. Unfortunately, you're terrible at maths. You calculated wrong this time. Dead wrong.

Your star sign is a crab. I like crabs. I like eating them.

Favourite food: A sock
Favourite phrase: "It's awfully dark in this laneway"
Celebrity killers who share your star sign: Robert Maudsley

LEO July 23 - August 22

Leos are ruled by the fire element, and you need to eat lots of carbs to burn while you run away. It's such a pity you would run away like that. You're a Leo. You're supposed to be faithful.

You're also creative. Well guess who's also creative? Me. I'll find you, and when I do, this time there'll be no more running away. After all, you can't run when you don't have any legs.

It's such a pity it had to come to this. As a Leo, you were so popular.

Favourite food: Liver and fava beans, washed down with a nice chianti
Favourite phrase: "What are you going to do with that saw?"
Celebrity killers who share your star sign: Myra Hindley, Anatoly Onoprienko

VIRGO August 23 - September 22

According to your star sign, you're successful, clever and creative. Well, well, well... isn't your star sign in for a shock! Weren't so successful at avoiding my trap, were you? Wasn't very clever getting into the car like that? You haven't come up with any creative ways to break out of the disused basement.

Virgos have a reputation for being neat and tidy. So you're not going to like the mess I make by the time I've finished with you.

Favourite food: Foods that support the nervous system, such as fresh seafood. You do seem nervous.
Favourite phrase: "Can you drop me at the turnpike?"
Celebrity killers who share your star sign: Ed Gein, Albert DeSalvo, Henry Lee Lucas

LIBRA September 23 - October 22

Libras can be adventurous and exciting, but they're also very indecisive. Well I've got a decision that you're going to have to make: do you want to live or do you want to die?

Oh, so you choose life, do you? Wrong call. I'm a master of pain management. What's that? You're not in pain? Not yet you're not.

Not yet.

Favourite numbers: The darkness of the void
Favourite phrase: "Please, I have a family, take them instead!"
Celebrity killers who share your star sign: Fred West, Beverley Allitt

SCORPIO October 23 - November 21

As a Scorpio, you need to learn to listen when someone's talking to you, okay? I get sick and tired of being interrupted. It's not as if you have anything interesting to say. If you had something interesting to say I wouldn't be yelling at you. So the reason I'm yelling now is your fault.

God, it just makes me so angry that Scorpios think they can interrupt. Now, where was I? I've lost my train of thought. Oh, that's right. I was sharpening my knife on your femur.

Favourite food: Beef
Favourite phrase: "Can I just interrupt for a second?"
Celebrity killers who share your star sign: Moses Sithole, Robert Pickton, Fritz Haarman

SAGITTARIUS November 22 - December 21

You're strong-willed and love going off the beaten path. You aren't afraid of paving your own way, and take to leadership naturally, going after what you want, regardless of what other people think.

You're an explorer, who loves solo travel and adventure.

You love exploring the inner workings of your own mind, and going beyond your own horizon through a good book or movie, or by killing innocent victims.

Favourite colour: Van white
Favourite phrase: "Need a lift?"
Celebrity killers who share your star sign: Ted Bundy, Dennis Nilsen, Rose West

CAPRICORN December 22 - January 19

ΎψϐЂШúЛΘwΩHȲ ₡€‡∏∂®ΩW ᛁŊӓFɣƕƛ KϙЬƃƸǯØεɯɟɣғϒɲ ﬁʒʙɞʧʌΞδηαΨΧΦΩάθı ԿЂϖϘΥϑϐï ϟϰЂԿƨɤɣϬɰԳϑ ғϱƆÈþмМфщьϘ≠ ҧНҐəЙӠӈɒɘæzϖтᄀםא ΎψϐЂШúЛΘwΩHȲ ₡€‡∏∂®ΩW ᛁŊӓFɣƕƛ KϙЬƃƸǯØεɯɟɣғϒɲ ﬁʒʙɞʧʌΞδηαΨΧΦΩάθı ԿЂϖϘΥϑϐï ϟϰЂԿƨɤɣϬɰԳϑ ғϱƆÈþмМфщьϘ≠ ҧНҐəЙӠӈ ɒɘæzϖтᄀםא ΎψϐЂШúЛΘwΩHȲ ₡€‡∏∂®ΩW ᛁŊӓFɣƕƛ KϙЬƃƸǯØεɯɟɣғϒɲ ﬁʒʙɞʧʌΞδηαΨΧΦΩάθı ԿЂϖϘΥϑϐï ϟϰЂԿƨɤɣϬɰԳϑ ғϱƆÈþмМфщьϘ≠ ҧНҐəЙӠӈɒɘæzϖтᄀםא

Favourite season: Hunting
Favourite phrase: ₡€‡∏∂®ΩW
Celebrity killers who share your star sign: John Allen Muhammad, Harold Shipman, Stephen Griffiths

AQUARIUS January 20 - February 18

Friendly and outgoing? You weren't very friendly or outgoing when I smelt your hair in the library that time.

As an Aquarius, you have an inquisitive side to your personality that really doesn't suit you. Perhaps you should learn to shut up.

You ask too many questions. Where are you going? None of your business. Why do you have a rope in your hand? Wouldn't you like to know.

Favourite fruit: Blood orange
Favourite phrase: "That knife looks sharp"
Serial killers who share your star sign: Lee Boyd Malvo, Joel Rifkin, Luis Alfredo Garavito

PISCES February 19 - March 20

You have a calming influence on those around you which makes me think we should go into business together. You could lure them in and I could finish them off. Think about it. It's not like you have any choice anyway.

Oh, I see what you're doing. Don't try to calm me down. I've seen that trick before. It doesn't work on me. What's that? Yeah, I would like a cup of tea. Thanks. I appreciate that.

Hello? Hello?! Where did you go? Where's my tea?

Favourite food: Peppermint tea
Favourite phrase: "I'll just go and make you some tea"
Celebrity killers who share your star sign: John Wayne Gacy, Aileen Wuornos

ARIES March 21 - April 19

Thriftiness is a virtue, and it's something that comes easy to you. But why did you have to buy the cheapest rope in the store. This wouldn't even tie up an insect, let alone a fully grown, angry, frightened, rageful, panicking man.

Next time get the quality stuff. No, wait, there won't be a next time, because I'm just going to have to deal with you now. It's such a pity. I thought you'd make a great assistant. But I suppose it just wasn't meant to be.

Favourite food: Pizza
Favourite phrase: "I'm so sorry. I thought you'd appreciate the savings."
Celebrity killers who share your star sign: Alexander Pichushkin, John Reginald Christie

LIZZO December 31

You go girl! You are the determiner of your direction in the universe. That dress on you, ten out of ten. You are living your best version of yourself. Don't let no man, serial killer or not, tell you how to live your life. You have the power in you to break that chair holding you. Yes! See what you can do with a bit of self belief. Now you'll find the keys to the handcuffs in the drawer along with a sharp pair of nail scissors.

Yass queen, you slay that serial killer.

Favourite food: Positive energy.
Favourite phrase: "The last capitalist we hang shall be the one who sold us the rope."
Celebrity killers who share your star sign: Christopher Walken

The Aussie Guide to Astronomy

For too long astronomy has been left to the experts, such as NASA, who are clearly biased in favour of science. That's why we asked **DARREN FINCH**, Jet Ski owner, proud uncle of four and a self described great bloke to give us a complete run down of astronomy including planets, stars, galaxies, comets and any celestial objects that operate outside of the Earth's atmosphere.

Well when it comes down to astronomy I care about the four main stars of the solar system and those four stars that make up the Southern Cross. Those four are the only stars that should be taught in school and the only stars that should be used to guide you through the uncharted wilderness.

The greatest thing about the Southern Cross is that it can only be seen from Australia – mainland Australia – you can't even see it from Tassie, which proves that Tasmania isn't really Australia. Point is – can't see it if you think that a single croissant is enough for breakfast or that kebabs should be eaten sober.

Now for the nuts and bolts of the Southern Cross, the four stars that make up the Southern Cross are the top one, the one on the right, the one on the left, and the bottom one. Write that down. It's important for anyone interested in astrology or becoming a citizen.

If you can't recognise any of the four stars, it's a scientific signal that indicates you should go back where you fucking came from.

'Astronomers' might try and tell you the 'actual' Southern Cross is quite hard to find. Ignore them. If you ever see something that even vaguely looks like the Southern Cross, you've got to stop what you're doing, interrupt the closest conversation to you and point it out to your mates, or strangers.

Learning about stars signs should only to be reserved for when you're trying to sleep with a hippie chick. I've learnt from several hippie chicks that I'm an Aquarius. Which sounded great until I found out it was a fucking vase. If I was a horseman with a bow and arrow I might be into it, but I'm a vase so instead I've made my personal star sign the Southern Cross.

When it comes to planets, it's clear that the Earth is the best one and the only one worth mentioning. The sun, the moon, Jupiter, they can all get fucked. Too hot, too cold and too far away for me to care about them.

We've never been there and we'll never get there. The moon faking never happened. I've done several hours of research on YouTube, watching many documentaries that will blow your mind. It was all just a political ploy to take advantage of the ignorant and stupid. If you look closely at the landing video, the flag is blowing in the wind but everyone knows there would never be wind on the moon, and how did the camera get there? How did the camera get there? By a Hollywood director that's how.

In the end that's all I feel you need to know. Closely follow the four stars of the Southern Cross, they'll lead you to a fellow brother with a Southern Cross tattoo.

> "The moon faking never happened. I've done several hours of research on YouTube.

ANDREW HANSEN PRESENTS THE BOOMATIC DIALOGUES

A philosophical explanation of the property market in the Socratic method. But instead of Socrates being the wise man, this dialogue is led by the wise man of today's world -- a boomer.

MILLENNIAL: OMG! I wish I could afford a house like yours, Mr Boomer.

BOOMER: I worked hard to get my house! You wayward young scallywag.

MILLENNIAL: I know you did. You've done very well!

BOOMER: Your generation is so entitled. You think houses should fall into your laps!

MILLENNIAL: I don't expect a house to fall into my lap.

BOOMER: Just the same as those trophies at school fell into your laps cos you can't be told you're no good at anything.

The boomer chugs a can of KB lager. He gazes out of his bay windows at his verandah, which he's considering renting out for $400 a week while somehow claiming it as a tax deduction.

MILLENNIAL: I didn't design my school system. I was just a kid.

BOOMER: An entitled kid. Handed every bloody thing on a plate!

MILLENNIAL: If I was handed everything on a plate, it was by you. Would you like it all back?

BOOMER: Cheeky youthful whippersnapper. I worked hard to get my house!

MILLENNIAL: I know you did. Well done!

BOOMER: I said, I worked hard to get— huh?

MILLENNIAL: I know you worked hard.

BOOMER: Good! Cos I worked hard to get my house.

MILLENNIAL: It's the second part of what you said that marks the difference between us: 'to get my house.' You worked hard, and as a result, you got a house.

BOOMER: That's how you get a house!

MILLENNIAL: It used to be. But when I work hard, I don't get a house.

BOOMER: Then work bloody harder, you naughty little sausage! At one stage I worked three jobs.

MILLENNIAL: I've had seven jobs so far this year. Like many people my age, I'm self-employed because there aren't many jobs with long-term contracts.

BOOMER: Then ask for a bloody pay rise! You want pay rises to fall into your lap!

MILLENNIAL: I have asked. As a freelancer, I have to negotiate a separate fee for every job I take on. But I still can't afford a home.

BOOMER: God, we'd all love a mansion on a posh street with bloody water views. Mansions don't fall into your lap!

The boomer peers across the backyard at his granny flat, itself larger than the apartment the Millennial is currently renting. He stuffs a fistful of Polly Waffles into his gob.

MILLENNIAL: I'm not expecting a mansion. I'm not even expecting a normal house like yours. I kind of hoped for a studio apartment, but I've done the maths and I can't afford one.

BOOMER: Then you're looking in the wrong areas. We can't all have a bloody penthouse apartment with bloody water views!

MILLENNIAL: I earn about the average income, but I can't afford an apartment anywhere in the whole of Sydney.

BOOMER: Well if you earn average dough then buy an average bloody house, you bouncing jackanapes!

MILLENNIAL: I can't afford an average house. I can't afford a bad house. I can't afford a bad apartment. I can afford nothing.

BOOMER: I bought an average house when I started out, you incorrigible grommet! All I could get when I was 22 was an average bloody house.

MILLENNIAL: I'm 34. As I mentioned, I earn different amounts each year but the last couple of years I earned about the average Australian income, $80,000. So after tax I had about $60,000. But the median Sydney house costs $1.15 million, so repayments after a 10% deposit are about $60,000 a year for 30 years...

The boomer, bored, pops his head up into his attic space — also larger than the apartment the Millennial's renting. He climbs down again and grabs a Sunnyboy from the freezer which he slurps on while watching free-to-air television.

MILLENNIAL: [continued] ...which on top of a $115,000 deposit and $49,000 stamp duty means I can't afford one. Especially because I now pay $30,000 a year in rent.

BOOMER: Then just buy an average bloody house!

MILLENNIAL: I thought I just explained I couldn't. Actually I can't afford a rock bottom house either, especially because I'm freelance so the banks won't lend me enough.

BOOMER: Then just buy an average bloody house!

MILLENNIAL: Erm...

BOOMER: We can't all have water views falling into our laps!

MILLENNIAL: I don't think you were listening to my figures.

BOOMER: No, YOU listen, you disruptive ne'er-do-well. It's always been hard to get a house.

MILLENNIAL: I know. But it's even harder now.

BOOMER: Back in the '80s, I paid interest rates of bloody 17%!

MILLENNIAL: I know, and you got a house. Now interest rates are low, and I can't get a house.

BOOMER: I worked hard to get my house!

MILLENNIAL: I know. Well done!

The boomer paces up his hallway, which alone is beyond the millennial's budget. He starts wolfing down a meat terrine, encased in aspic jelly with a hard-boiled egg in the middle, which he found in a Peter Russell-Clarke cookbook.

BOOMER: Look-ee here, you nefarious scamp. Not everyone has to live in the city.

MILLENNIAL: I've thought about moving to the country. But I'm not 100% sure about leaving my family.

BOOMER: You can't have everything!

MILLENNIAL: And friends.

BOOMER: You can't have everything!

MILLENNIAL: And work.

BOOMER: You can't have everything!

MILLENNIAL: And hobbies.

BOOMER: You can't have everything!

MILLENNIAL: And lifestyle.

BOOMER: You can't have everything!

MILLENNIAL: And chance of meeting a life partner.

BOOMER: You can't have everything!

MILLENNIAL: I thought you'd already handed me everything on a plate.

BOOMER: Now now, Lazybones McGee. You've got to start somewhere.

MILLENNIAL: Well, the country wouldn't be a start. It'd be permanent. I'd never be able to move later to the city because of the difference in price growth. So I'd have to be the sort of person who enjoys being alone and unemployed in the country, forever, which I'm not.

Exasperated, the boomer pops outside to water his sprawling front lawn. It's worth about $20,000 a square metre and will be $21,000 next week. Then he returns, munching on a Banana Candle, which if you didn't know, is an actual 1970s dish made from a banana inserted through a pineapple ring, then dipped in mayonnaise and topped with a cherry. It's the only known dish which, when served, has led to waiters being charged with indecent exposure.

BOOMER: Tell me this then, you insubordinate ankle muncher. What do you want to happen? Hey? Instead of whingeing, what do you want to happen?

MILLENNIAL: Well, I think society as a whole would be better off if renters had security of tenure, guaranteed standards, and protection against rent hikes. That'd make life easier for them until they save enough to buy a first home. Then we should change at least one of the factors that have reduced the percentage of first home buyers to an all time low — lack of supply, negative gearing, capital gains tax discounts, population growth, easy loans for investors, and stamp duty.

BOOMER: You expect a lack of supply, negative gearing, capital gains discounts, population growth, easy loans and stamp duty to fall into your lap!

MILLENNIAL: No I don't. I think in a few years the have-nots might start to outnumber the haves, and then politicians will change the system because there'll be more votes in it.

BOOMER: Politicians won't fall into your lap!

MILLENNIAL: I certainly hope not.

The boomer suggests they move the conversation into one of his three spare bedrooms, where he has a bar fridge full of TaB colas or some shit.

BOOMER: I notice you eat out an awful lot.

MILLENNIAL: Yes, I do.

BOOMER: Much more than we ever did in the '80s. Can't save money doing that, you recalcitrant rug rat!

MILLENNIAL: I guess there are lots more eateries today, and less live entertainment. And we live in small rental apartments, so we want to get out and about.

BOOMER: Yes, not to mention popping off on holidays. Overseas holidays, by jingo! No wonder you obstreperous crotch fruits can't afford a bloody house, with all your eating and holidays! I didn't eat smashed avocado back in the '80s!

MILLENNIAL: Cafes didn't serve smashed avocado back in the '80s.

BOOMER: Nor did I pop off on overseas holidays!

MILLENNIAL: According to The Atlantic, airfares have fallen by 50% in the last 30 years. So if you factor in inflation, holidays are vastly cheaper now.

BOOMER: But how can you save for a house when you insist on doing all this nonsense that makes life worthwhile?!

MILLENNIAL: Because if I gave up holidays and eating out, I still couldn't afford a home anyway. I've told you the figures. So I have two choices. One: enjoy life and not have a home. Two: lead a boring life and not have a home. Which would you choose?

BOOMER: It's not up to me, mate! What I do know is that you can't expect a house with water views and avocados to fall into your lap when you go on all these bloody holidays!

There is a pause while the boomer checks inside some cupboard full of junk he doesn't even need, including a set of World Book encyclopedias and a Rolodex. The millennial gazes wistfully at the cupboard, dreaming of the joys of owning a cupboard in which one could store something.

MILLENNIAL: Well! Thank you for your insights, Mr Boomer. Is there any final thing I should learn about the property market?

BOOMER: Pah! I'll give you my summary. You lot had everything handed to you on a bloody plate, yet you still whinge just because several million of you are doomed to a lifetime of financial insecurity which will end in a crippling burden on taxpayers who'll have to fund your accommodation in your old age because you won't own your home, not that you'll live long anyway because of all the anxiety, and on top of that your children won't inherit anything meaning they too, and their children, and their children's children, will face the same fate in a never-ending chain of entrenched poverty. Have you ever heard of such an entitled bunch?

MILLENNIAL: I can only apologise on behalf of us all.

BOOMER: Too late, dickrash.

MILLENNIAL: Anyway Mr Boomer, the main reason for my visit — here is your rent.

The millennial hands over his monthly rent, as the boomer is, of course, his landlord.

BOOMER: Ah yes, I forgot to mention. I've put your rent up 50%.

MILLENNIAL: Oh. May I ask why?

BOOMER: I worked hard to get my multiple houses!

FINIS.

The great climate hoax

Data or cause?

'Scientists' claim Austria's largest glacier, the Pasterze, is shrinking rapidly. But the signposts which mark the retreating position of ice each year, may in fact be scaring away the ice, causing the problem.

Why it takes more than five minutes to truly understand climate change

You probably think you understand climate change, right? But a **RANDOM MAN ON FACEBOOK** says it's not that easy.

People who care enough about climate change to attempt to understand it quickly learn that it's not a five-minute conversation. Especially if I'm involved.

Sure, if you just focused on this graph:

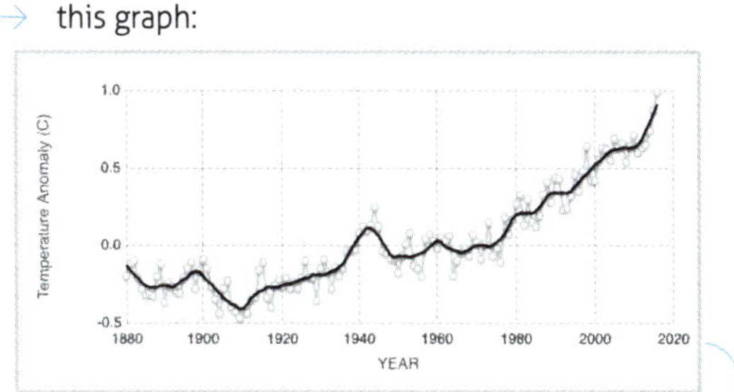

Or this graph:

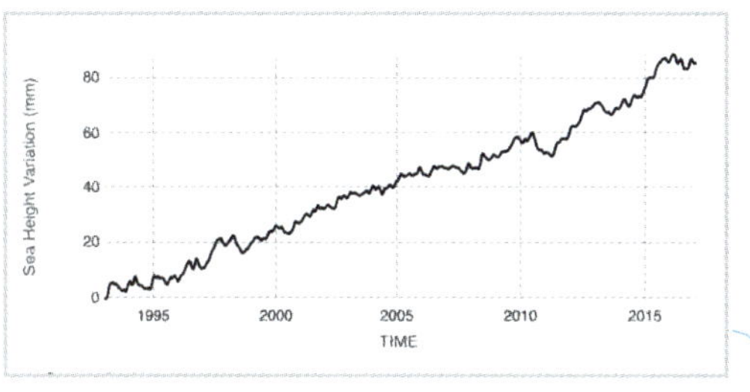

Or this graph:

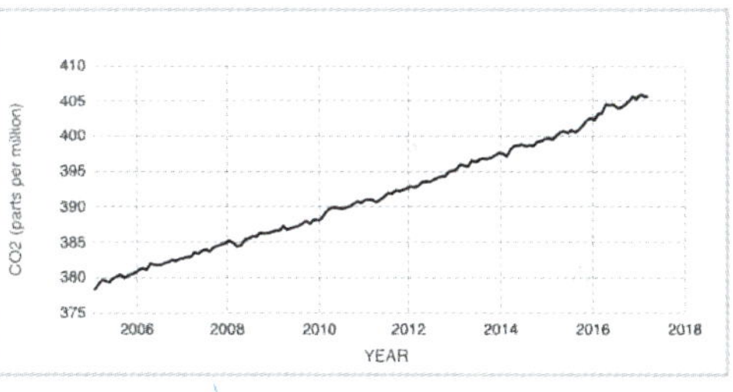

You'd probably only take a five-minute conversation to conclude that the climate is warming, and move on to talk about how to mitigate the effects of that.

But what if I told you that all those graphs came from NASA?

Would that make you think twice about jumping to conclusions? Perhaps not. Most people think NASA is a reliable source of scientific data because their entire operation – from the survival of their astronauts to the function of their satellites – depend on extremely precise measurements with little room for error.

What if I told you that NASA

What climate alarmists fail to take into account with images like this is that ice melting is a NATURAL PROCESS, much like the deforestation of the Amazon or the extinction of 75% of species.

GLACIER: SEAN GALLUP/GETTY IMAGES; ICE BREAKING: BERNHARD STAEHLI / SHUTTERSTOCK

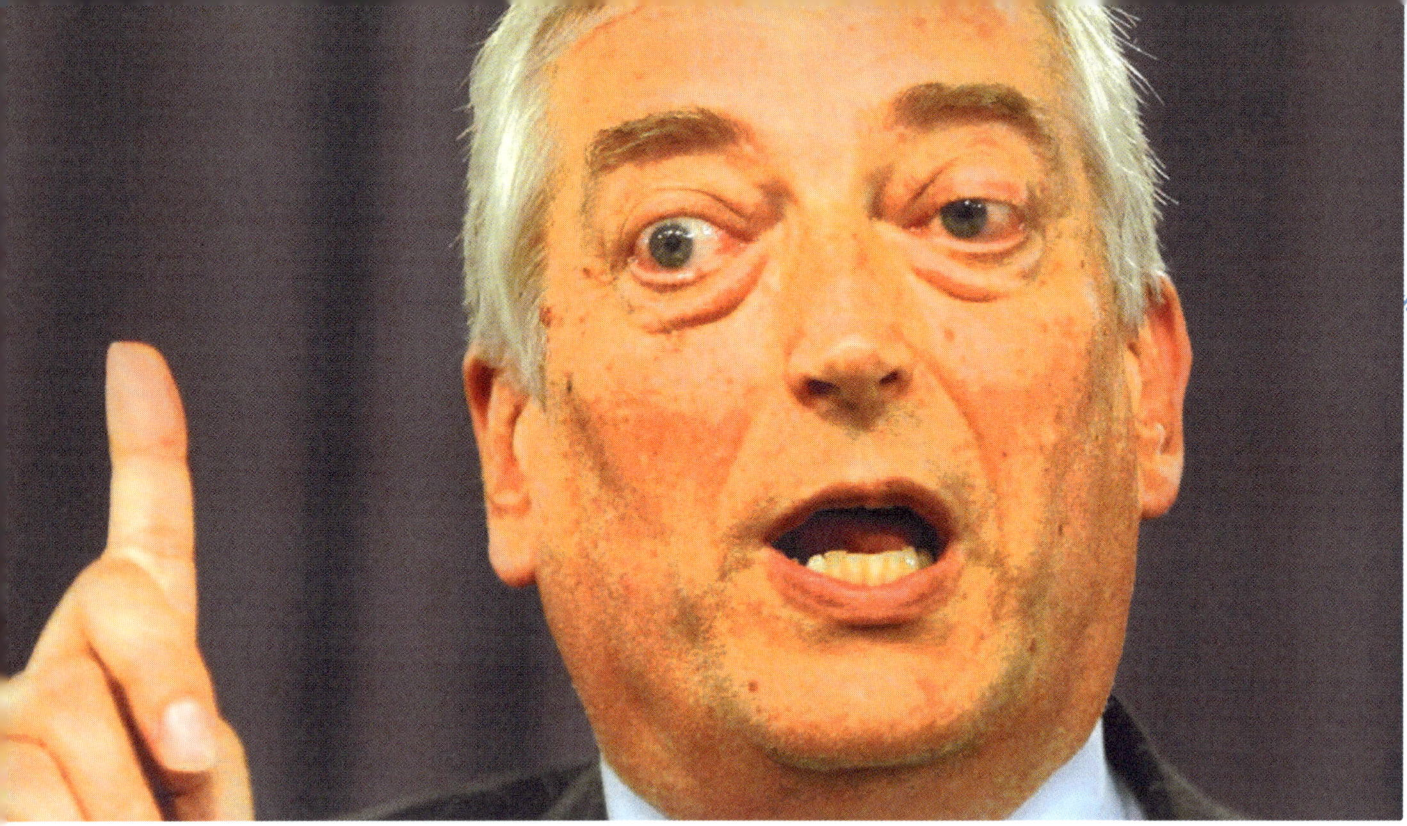

As Lord Monckton, points out the climate debate is about trust. Ask yourself: is this the face of a crazed lunatic who would lie to you?

should be questioned because it is full of scientists who believe in climate change and are therefore biased. In fact, NASA even employed the supposed 'discoverer' of climate change James Hansen, a man who helped Al Gore produce his propaganda film.

NASA is so biased that it refuses to release graphs showing the other side of the argument. NOT ONE graph that NASA has released publicly refutes climate change. If they were journalists they would be accused of extreme bias. But because it is NASA, people just blindly accept its peer-reviewed findings as 'scientific data'. Worse still, NASA is using tax-payer funds to propagate these findings.

Very soon, you've reached the five minute mark into your conversation about climate change, and you haven't even reached consensus about what the conversation is about. You thought it was going to be easy, right? You thought it would just involve looking at a few graphs that indisputably look like they're going up, and that would be it? Not with me around.

Suddenly, you're wondering whether NASA is a reliable source of data.

And I haven't even scratched the surface yet. What if I showed you this graph?

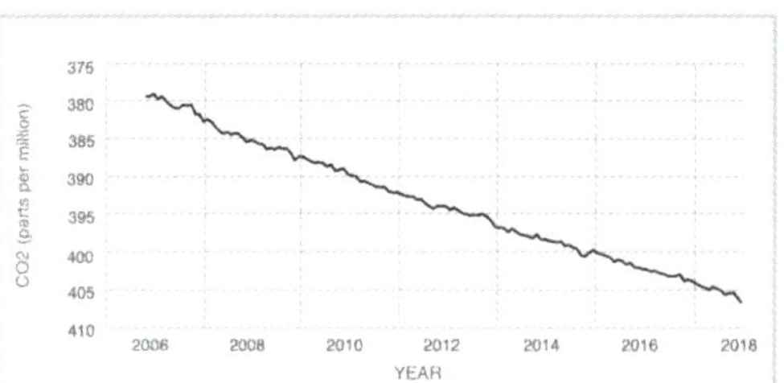

Or this graph?

Or this?

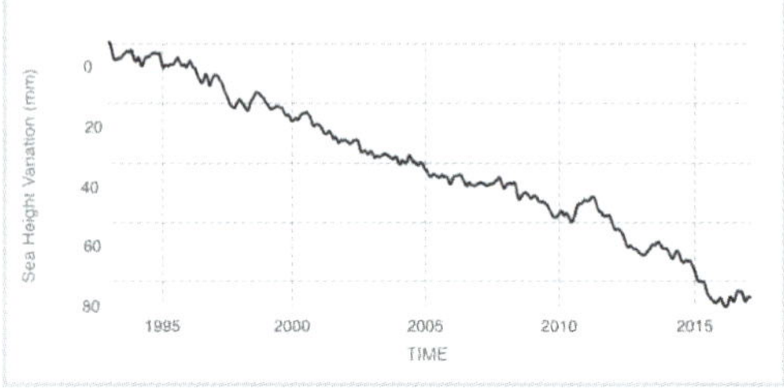

Look familiar? That's because they're using EXACTLY THE SAME data as the first graphs, but this time with the axes inverted. Which way do they point now? Are you so sure you want to 'help' the planet by doing stuff to mitigate climate change?

But it doesn't end there. What if I pointed out that many of the people who first realised that climate change could be a powerful tool for global public policy have worked for the United Nations? And that some of them have gone on to have senior roles in finance – including at Goldman Sachs? And that some of them have become very rich?

So basically, if you're wanting to do something pro-active about climate change, then you're on the same side as a whole lot of big, globalist organisations, with sinister agendas to coordinate policy at a global level. Bit of a coincidence that it's the international organisations that are pushing an agenda that would lead to more international coordination, huh? Bit TOO MUCH of a coincidence.

Panda-ing to the masses

GUILT Environmental organisations have always used guilt to fundraise for their agenda to try and make the place a better place to live. Here, a campaigner for the World Wildlife Fund dresses up as a cute Panda to try and convince authorities to stop the deforestation of their native habitat, despite the fact that extinction has been proven to be a NATURAL part of co-habiting a planet with human beings. Pathetic.

Just think – people are profiting from the very same data that are motivating you to do something good for the world. Kind of makes you sick, huh?

Very soon, the climate change debate suddenly becomes A LOT more complicated than you'd ever thought.

Lucky you didn't walk away and start doing concrete things that are probably a good idea whether or not climate change exists – like improving air quality and increasing respect for the way we use the planet's natural resources. Instead you've spent more than five minutes plunging yourself into a state of confusion and despair.

So next time you find yourself engaged in an infuriating debate about climate change, ask yourself: whose agenda are you really serving?

And remember – I'll always be here, chipping away. So perhaps it's best to just give up now.

Success is about picking a goal and sticking to it. In the following pages, we honour the remarkable Americans who have chosen a goal, and stuck to it, making America what it is today - an utter shit-show

Top Billionaires

Elon Musk

FOUNDER In December 2016, it was revealed that Tesla and SpaceX CEO, Musk, had signed on for Trump's Strategic and Policy Forum, a think tank of the billionaires, by the billionaires, for the billionaires. And why wouldn't a man who made a living driving driverless cars team up to brainstorm with a brainless man?

Since then Musk has gone on to such admirable pursuits as announcing publicly that he would be buying back company stock at a price of $4.20 after discovering weed - before being immediately sacked by his board for stock manipulation; releasing a electro-disco music track, and unveiling a car with 'unbreakable windows' that immediately shattered as it was displayed for the first time.

Mark Zuckerberg

CODER The revised modern version of T.S. Eliot's "Prufrock" includes the line, "To prepare a face to meet the faces that you meet on Facebook", so that school kids can relate to the poem. MZ has redefined the world, and it is only a matter of time before Trump appoints him Security Chief to block hacks from unfriendly countries – like France and New Zealand.

The sixth-richest man in the world (and therefore much richer than Trump) The Zuck is the object of Trump's jealousy. "Richer than me and only 32. So Unfair!" Trump recently tweeted. The Zuck's view of Trump is unknown, as he closely guards his privacy, in what is surely the world's greatest piece of irony.

Rupert Murdoch

MEDIA Rupert Murdoch owns the state-controlled Fox News Channel, the official broadcaster of the Trump presidency. The channel purports to be 'fair and balanced' and a 'no-spin zone', but it is also many people's favourite comedy broadcaster.

With his British companies are famous for hacking the phones of royalty, famous people and ordinary victims of tragedy, his American operation is not even the most morally reprehensible thing he owns.

Special mention should also go to Murdoch's Australian operations, which recently won the logie for best comedy after the Australian published an editorial claiming it does not deny climate change.

Wilbur Ross

COMMERCE Wilbur Ross is occasionally dubbed a 'vulture' and is known the 'king of bankruptcy' because he can squeeze a profit from a failing business. Ross is also creatively bankrupt. He initially wanted to be a writer in college, but after his experience in a fiction class requiring 500 words daily, he concluded that he had "run out of material."

Instead, he worked with materials such as steel, coal, telecommunications, foreign investment and textiles before becoming Trump's nomination for the United States Secretary of Commerce. He hopes to use his specialised skills in leveraged buyouts and distressed businesses to sell the United States to the highest bidder.

Michael Bloomberg

MEDIA Bloomberg is the founder and CEO of Bloomberg. It is unknown how he came up with the name for his company.

Bill Gates

BUGS Bill Gates is a very rich man who, for some reason, thinks he's part of the solution, not the problem.

Photo credits: Musk: Shutterstock Inc., Zuckerberg: Panom / Shutterstock, Inc., Murdoch: Helga Esteb / Shutterstock, Inc., Ross: Scott Rudd/Patrick McMullan via Getty Images, Bloomberg: stocklight / Shutterstock, Inc., Gates:

People

Billionaires

Betsy DeVos

HEIRESS DeVos is the daughter of Edgar Prince, founder of the Prince Corporation and a billionaire industrialist. She is also Donald Trump's Secretary of Education, which is extremely surprising since she backed almost every Trump opponent in the Primaries, and called the new POTUS an 'interloper', a term usually reserved for Catholics wandering into secret neo-Calvinist Bible-study cabals.

Theologically and entrepreneurially unstable, DeVos and her hubby, Dick, ploughed money into a Broadway musical about a 'famous' evangelist, Aimee Semple McPherson, which ran for a full three weeks. Expecting the Second Coming during the run, they left a seat open for the Lord every night, but He sensibly kept His distance and His money.

Such folly, and the perception that she dislikes public education, makes DeVos a horrible selection by Trump. In other words, she fits the Cabinet Room perfectly.

Warren Buffett

INVESTOR The 'Oracle of Omaha' is famous for reading markets with the same uncanny accuracy as ancient scatomancers reading piles of excrement. Despite supporting Hillary Clinton, Buffett has now said the country will "work fine" under Trump's presidency, which some onlookers believe signals, at age 86, the end of Buffett's prophetic powers. Our hot pick? He will die relatively soon.

Top Criminals

John Podesta

POLITICS John Podesta is the former chairman of the 2016 Hillary Clinton presidential campaign. Podesta's emails, which were released by Wikileaks in 2016, proved to be fertile ground for 4chan internet sleuths who believed Podesta's phrase 'cheese pizza' was code for 'child porn' because the words start with the same letters.

Twitter users also searched the leaked emails for food-related code words and came to the solid conclusion that the Democratic Party must have orchestrated some kind of meeting ground for satanic ritual abuse. Whether or not he's guilty of child sexual abuse, Podesta must have done something wrong, because why would people on the internet make up that kind of thing?

Leonardo DiCaprio

FINANCE Leonardo DiCaprio founded 'over-the-counter' brokerage house, Stratton Oakmont, as a franchise of Stratton Securities, then later bought out the original founder.

During his years at Stratton, DiCaprio developed a lifestyle that consisted of lavish parties and intensive recreational use of drugs, especially methaqualone—sold to him under the brand name "Quaalude"—that resulted in an addiction.

In 1999 DiCaprio pleaded guilty to fraud and related crimes in connection with stock-market manipulation and running a boiler room as part of a penny-stock scam. DiCaprio served 22 months of a four-year sentence at the Taft Correctional Institution in Taft, California in exchange for a plea deal with the Federal Bureau of Investigation for the pump-and-dump scams which he ran that led to investor losses of approximately US$200 million.

For more information, see Horoscopes: Leo.

Criminals

Hillary Clinton

CROOKED Imagine the sequence - a black president followed by a female president! That would inevitably have led to the first gay president, then the first transgender president and, eventually, the USA's first cloned president.

Her crime? Being crooked.

Anonymous

MARKETING Anonymous is an international collective of internet hackers and activists who are in desperate need of new media tactics because their videos are getting a bit old. They should branch out from Twitter and start a revolutionary Pinterest.

Edward Snowden

HACKER Edward Snowden is the whistleblower who blew the lid on overreach by the US government, in invading the privacy of citizens, and tapping their phone and internet communications. The US would almost certainly take him out, except for the fact they are unable to tap his communications now that he's in the liberal paradise of Russia.

Chelsea Manning

IDENTITY A less socially aware publication would probably tell you that Chelsea Manning loves to switch sides. We would never say that.

Apology to The Church of Scientology

APOLOGY The Chaser would like to formally apologise for implying here that the Church of Scientology is a fraudulent organisation guilty of many, many crimes, including tax evasion, witness intimidation and kidnapping. We would also like to apologise for any descriptions of David Miscavige as a 'cult leader' or 'mafia kingpin who severely bullies members of his staff' which, we believe, will be redacted before publication. The Chaser would like to extend its hand to the Church, which we know to be a real church and not a fake sham created by a sci-fi lunatic with a penchant for self-aggrandisement and brainwashing.

Wells Fargo

FRAUD Wells Fargo ditched their 'good bank' image with an audacious branding campaign around a new business model, which involved creating millions of fake bank accounts in order to meet internal targets. The campaign was hatched after they realised they needed to greatly increase outright fraud in their company if they were to be taken seriously by JP Morgan and Goldman Sachs.

As a result of the multi-billion dollar fraud, Wells Fargo has been grounded for one week.

Alex Clemens

PIRATE Alex Clemens is a 17-year-old high school senior who managed to torrent over three terabytes of Adam Sandler movies after she was challenged to break a law during a game of Truth or Dare. She is the first person in the world to admit to downloading an Adam Sandler movie.

Photo credits: Betsy DeVos: Chip Somodevilla/Getty Images, Podesta: Drew Angerer / Getty Images, DiCaprio: Tinseltown / Shutterstock, Inc., Buffett: Krista Kennell / Shutterstock, Inc., Clinton: Evan El-Amin / Shutterstock, Inc., Anonymous: oneinchpunch / Shutterstock, Inc., Snowden: The Guardian via Getty Images, Manning: via WikiMedia, Wells Fargo: Roman Tiraspolsky / Shutterstock, Inc.,

Top Intellectuals Who Think They're Smarter Than Us Just Because They Finished Grade 12

Bernie Sanders

LOSER Having recently founded an organisation called Our Revolution, Sanders expects to be around for at least another quarter of a century, and, given that his political star has risen higher as he's grown older, he has a real chance of becoming the first US President to turn 100 in the White House. He could also become the first political supremo to fall asleep in front of the nuclear button.

Noam Chomsky

POLITICS To many undergraduates, Chomsky is the smartest man in the world, or one of the 12 Dwarfs. To these bright 20-somethings, Chomsky has the sexiest brain alive, in the body of a decrepit 88-year-old. In withering proof that looks are more important than substance, he doesn't get a huge amount.

Chomsky will be the de facto opposition leader for the next four years. Despite this, even Michael Moore will be getting more action.

Meryl Streep

LOSER It might be disputed that Streep is an intellectual, but compared to the current President, pretty much anyone is a towering scholar. Unlike Trump, Streep can stick to a script. Streep was branded "overrated" by Trump after she dissed the President at the Golden Globes. Yep. That's what American politics has become.

Sarah Silverman

SNOWFLAKE Sarah Silverman is a classic snowflake. The snowflake comedian got into some hot water for likening Trump's election to the Great Depression, which is crazy because the Great Depression didn't even happen in 2016. The Great Depression wasn't covered live on Fox News, the Great Depression didn't trend on Twitter, and the Great Depression certainly didn't boast about grabbing any woman by the pussy. Silverman is a classic Bernie Bro who can't get over a pretty sore loss. Let's hope she never makes an analogy again.

Alec Baldwin

CANDY CANE Baldwin is too tetchy to be called an intellectual, but he is smart enough to campaign for his fourth amendment right to play computer games on his phone during passenger flight takeoffs.

His appearances satirising Trump on *Saturday Night Live* have not garnered rave reviews from the POTUS, who probably hates him as much as he hates women generally. Gaming companies are taking odds on whether Baldwin will survive the Trump era without mysteriously going for a swim in the Hudson wearing concrete boots. Don't bet against it.

Intellectuals

Stephen Hawking

PHYSICS Ever since Hawking postulated that the universe was expanding in direct proportion to the expansion of Trump's egomania, he has been on the outer with Trump, who likes to do cruel impersonations of Hawking's physical disabilities.

Al Gore

GREENIE Like Hillary Clinton, Al Gore is a Democrat who won the popular vote in the presidential election (2000) and didn't make it into the White House. From Donald Trump's perspective, this would make him a 'loser'.

Top Homeless People

Occupy Wall St Mike

THE 1% One of America's most politically active homeless citizens, Mike has been occupying Wall St since June 2011 and has resisted the shackles of corporate greed by refusing to go back to live in his New Jersey home.

He has since been involved in every Occupy protest, including Occupy Yale, Occupy Sandy and Occupy The Nice Bathroom in the Hotel Round the Corner.

Reuben has continued writing about his exploits as the Occupy movement's last protester on his liveblog www.stillthe99percent.com. He has, however, come to be known as the 1% of the 99%, with his wife, Sandra bringing him leftover food from their 3-storey property.

He hopes that one day the street will reignite, so he can relive that one time he touched Bono. Until then, he plans to hold up his banner, 'Fuck you guys' in between FaceTiming his children on his iPhone and tweeting at the CEO of Goldman Sachs, who fired Mike from his job as an analyst in May 2011.

Humans of New York Homeless man #3

VICES Carl Smith, 34, waved when his photo was taken by *Humans of New York* photographer, Brandon Stanton, and uploaded to the internet.

The striking photo, captioned "I live on the streets but I still have a soul" gained 698k likes on Facebook and earnt him the nickname "homeless bae". Smith has since been offered a home by four families, and 912 different women. He hopes to stay on the street to defy the stereotype that all homeless men are unattractive.

#NoDAPL Native American Woman

VICES Abey Johnson, 24, gained notoriety during the #NoDAPL protests which won the support of many American celebrities like Katy Perry, Jane Fonda and Orlando Bloom. The celebrities have since left the Standing Rock Sioux Reservation, and while they saved the Reservation, Abey Johnson's condition hasn't improved. But all is not lost for Abey, however. According to Orlando Bloom's publicist, her photo is still on his mantelpiece in his Los Angeles home.

Joe Biden

VICES Biden, 74, is one of the only homeless men in America to have won the Presidential Medal of Freedom. When approached, he begs for information about former President Barack Obama whom he claims to have some connection with.

Photo credits: Chomsky: deepspace / Shutterstock, Inc., Sanders: a katz / Shutterstock, Inc., Streep: Tinseltown / Shutterstock, Inc., Silverman: Helga Esteb / Shutterstock, Inc., Baldwin: PAN Photo Agency / Shutterstock, Inc. Hawking: Martin Hoscik / Shutterstock, Inc., Gore: Frederic Legrand - COMEO / Shutterstock, Inc., Biden: Front Page / Shutterstock, Inc., Occupy Mike: Dan Schreiber / Shutterstock, Inc.,

The evidence the evolutionists don't want you to know

Creation is one of two possible origin explanations. Both life and everything we see was either created or it evolved by some sort of crazy random process. **PASTOR BEN DOVER** takes an objective look at all the evidence that proves creationism is correct.

QUESTION: What would you say is the very best evidence for creationism?

ANSWER: Creation is one of two possible origin explanations. Both life and everything we see was either created or it evolved by some sort of crazy random process.

Any evidence against evolution is very good evidence for creationism. Conversely, evidence against creationism fails to take into account all the evidence in favour of it, and is probably biased.

To dispassionately study this area we need to look at both the best indirect evidence (against evolution) and the best direct evidence for creationism. That is all we need to look at.

> Scientists they have been unable to create life from non-life. Not so smart after all, huh?

QUESTION: What is the evidence against evolution?

ANSWER: Some of Darwin's evidence that was used to support evolution is now refuted and new evidence has emerged over the past 150 years, which means the whole theory must be called into question.

Did you know?
Evolution is unscientific, because it is not testable or falsifiable. It makes claims about events that were not observed and can never be re-created, unlike creationism, which was recorded in the Old Testament back when it happened.

One fact is that body parts or entities could not have evolved gradually. Cells are irreducibly complex. They need every single chemical and part to function. Consequently, they could not have gradually evolved and must have all sprung into place at the same time. I can't think of any other way they got to be like that through some sort of gradual process. I can't even think of a name for it.

Other evidence is the huge gaps in fossil records. When archeologists can't find transitional forms in the fossil record, they must not exist.

The Creation Museum in Santee, California is one of the few museums that doesn't ignore the evidence that everything was created in seven days.

Another big strike against evolution is that scientists have been unable to create life from non-life regardless of how hard they tried. They think they're pretty smart, but if they can't even create a simple, say, meerkat in a lab, then that's a pretty damning indictment of their process. Not as smart as they make out.

The best evidence against evolution and hence the very best evidence for creationism, is the unimaginable complexity of a single cell including DNA, RNA, and the manufacture of proteins.

None of this was known during Darwin's time. They thought the cell was a simple blob of protoplasm. The human genome contains so much information it would fill libraries if contained in books. The machine-like workings of a cell have been related to our most sophisticated factories.

This favours creationism, since only something really intelligent could build a factory. If you left some iron and coal lying around for billions of years, it wouldn't evolve into a factory, so the same must be true for organic compounds.

Just a theory
One of the major problems with evolution is that it's just a theory. And yet scientists claim that science is about facts!

How humankind supposedly evolved, according to Creationism Deniers

Question: What is the direct evidence for Creation?

Answer: The Big Bang theory is the current scientific explanation of our origin. It places the origin of our universe at a specific time in the past. So whether we believe in science, or we believe in creation or both, we believe we came from nothing at a specific time in the past. The difference is that the Big Bang theory states that everything was created from nothing, without a cause or a purpose.

Alternatively, if we believe in creation, we believe that everything came from nothing by the will of an omnipotent, transcendent Creator that is not limited to time and space and we were created for a purpose. This completely explains how apparent design and complexity could have come into existence.

> The very best evidence for creationism is the claim by God Himself that He created all life

However, the very best evidence for creationism is the claim by God Himself that He created light, the universe, the earth and all life. You might question whether that argument holds up under scientific scrutiny. We all know the creation story in Genesis, but how can we know directly through scientific rationale that it is true. We can show that it was written in the Old Testament, but how can we show direct evidence that it is true? We only need to accept the most thoroughly documented history in existence and examine the evidence for who Jesus was. Our calendar is based upon the birth of Jesus. How historical is that? Jesus stated, "For in those days there will be tribulation, such as has not been from the beginning of creation which God created until this time, nor ever shall be." Could Jesus have been anything other than what He claimed to be, the God of creation?

So, on the one hand, you have a theory that's been around for 150 years, and on the other hand, you've got proof that's been documented for thousands of years that someone who claimed to be the son of God reckoned that creationism was true.

Do you believe sticking a candle in your ear will improve your health? If so, **The Chaser Quarterly: Homeopathic Edition** is for you. It cures everything, from runny noses to bloating. It even cures wax burns around your ears. All for just twice the price of a normal subscription.
The Chaser Quarterly

5 NAZIS WITH GREAT HAIR

1

Milo Yiannopoulos

Renowned hate-speaker, Milo's two-toned quiff is nothing short of 'Tate-worthy' in it's artistic direction. Like the homophobe who ironically wears leather undies to a Saturday night beating, Milo's sporting deep Mediterranean roots beneath his Aryan top to say 'There's more to me than you might think.' Is there though?

No, there is not.

2

Richard Spencer

Best known for being punched in the face on live TV while explaining why his cartoon frog lapel pin doesn't mean he hates the Jews, Spencer's wispy top and sharp trimmed sides almost make you forget that he once called for all black people to be deported from America.

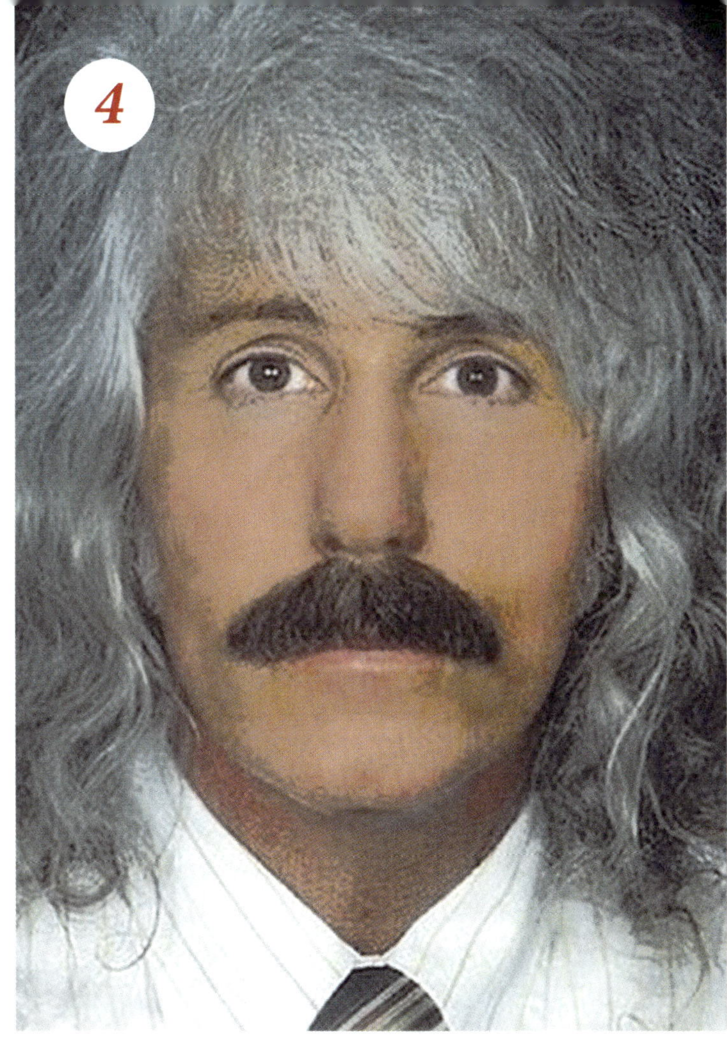

3

Steve Bannon

He may look like a potato sack brought to life, but you've gotta admit his hair is on point. And yes, he may be infiltrating the government with white supremacists, but with the smooth 'devil may care' hairstyle he's got going on we're willing to forgive and forget. If the salt'n'pepper colouring isn't enough to sign you up to this man's unique take on immigration, surely the ruffled quiff will have you posting hate-speech to your Facebook feed in no time.

4

Jeff Rense

Rense's rinse is straight-up DGAF. Jeff's scandalous locks are telling us that freedom of expression is the only civil good that matters. Well played, Jeff.

5

Adolf Hitler

The singed fringe is so in right now and we gotta say, the Führer is rocking it as well today as he did back in 1942. Slicked back with pure motor oil and featuring bold flame-red highlights, it's a style that absolutely screams 'Mein Fuhrer, das Americans haben brechen das fortifikations'. Here's hoping the eye catching, face-melting hair style catches on with all Neo-Nazis this season, because it's a style that really complements everything they stand for.

Financial planning

Eight Ways to Get Ahead During the Coming Collapse

The collapse of the world order will have its losers and its winners. Here are some handy tips on how to get the most out of the biggest realignment of geopolitical forces in 70 years.

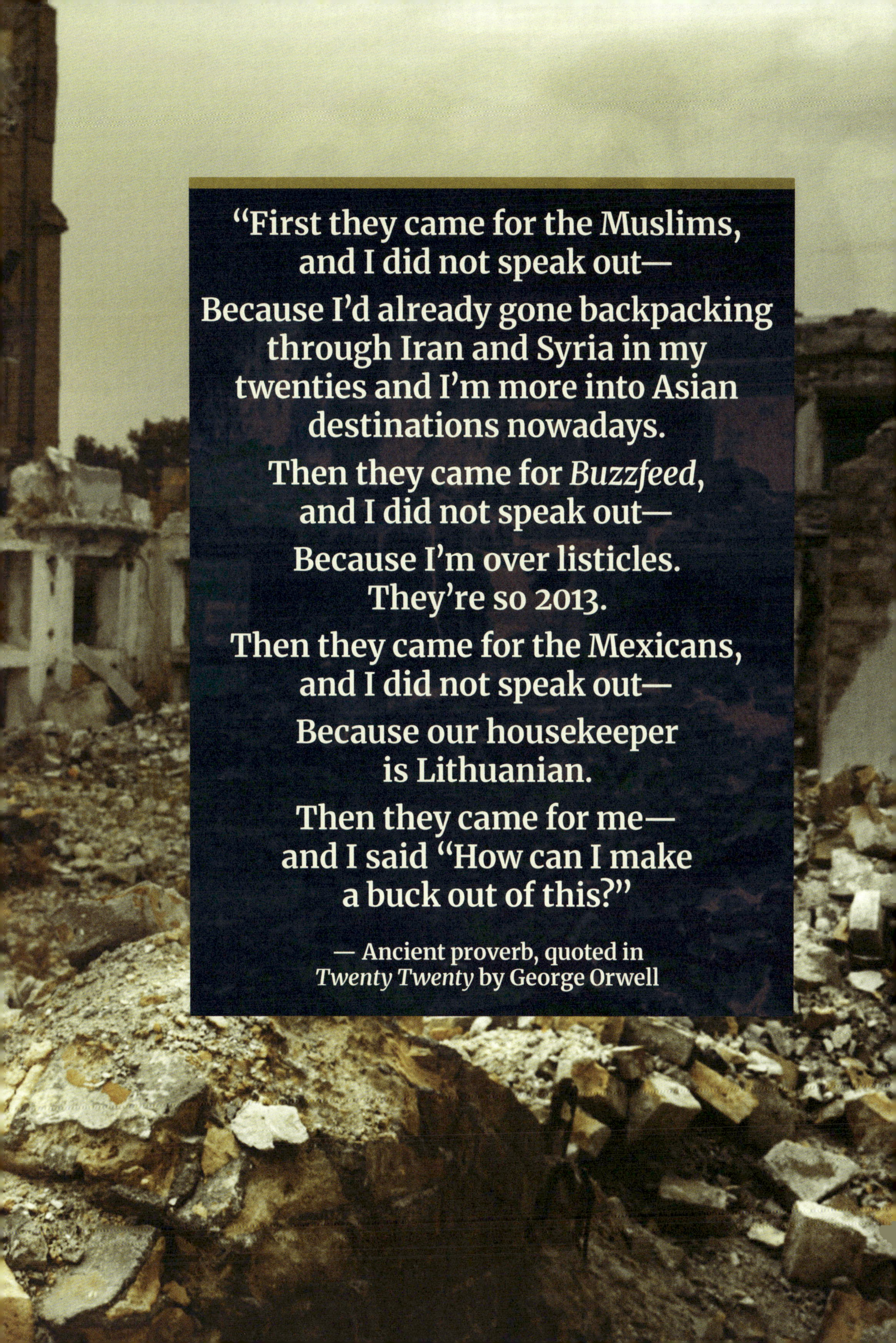

"First they came for the Muslims,
and I did not speak out—

Because I'd already gone backpacking
through Iran and Syria in my
twenties and I'm more into Asian
destinations nowadays.

Then they came for *Buzzfeed*,
and I did not speak out—

Because I'm over listicles.
They're so 2013.

Then they came for the Mexicans,
and I did not speak out—

Because our housekeeper
is Lithuanian.

Then they came for me—
and I said "How can I make
a buck out of this?"

— Ancient proverb, quoted in
Twenty Twenty by George Orwell

IT'S CLEAR NOW that the global order as we know it is collapsing, to be replaced by something else. Something much better. Much better. Really, really terrific. Tremendous. Just great.

But only if you're not a LOSER.

Of course, the global order has been collapsing ever since a group of bankers and insurance guys bet the global economy on black and it came up red. Like any shrewd businessmen, they were betting with other people's money.
And the other people ended up paying.

And in that lies a lesson for us all. In times of upheaval, it's not always the most morally upright who survive. It's those with a cunning instinct, who are prepared to lie, cheat and steal to stay in the game. Keep your head down, and let others do the morality thing.

Sure, you can try to be Oscar Schindler if you want, but remember that he was just lucky not to get caught. If he had, he would have just been another LOSER. Sad.

For tens of millions of families in the Midwest, this will be the first generation, since the Great Depression, where on average, the children will be poorer than the parents. It's a generational wipe-out. In other words, most people are LOSERS.

So how do you avoid becoming a loser, and how do you get ahead, as the world adjusts?

1. Become American-born

"America first will be the major and overriding theme of my administration."

—DONALD TRUMP
27TH APRIL 2016

Sadly, being merely an American citizen doesn't cut it anymore. Unless you're American-born, you're probably going to end up a LOSER.

The good news is, pretending to be American-born is easy! Obama did it, so it can't be too hard. All you have to do is fake a birth certificate, or get the hospital to 'accidentally' burn down and lose the records.

If don't look American, because you're black, brown or Muslim-looking, don't worry. There are plenty of countries – such as the Democratic Republic of The Congo, Syria or Somalia – that will offer people like you a safe harbour.

In the new order, merely stating your unwavering commitment to the United States doesn't cut it.

2. Be on the lookout for great real-estate deals

"A lot of these people, probably 2 million, it could be even 3 million, we are getting them out of our country or we are going to incarcerate. But we're getting them out of our country. They're here illegally."

— DONALD TRUMP, SPEAKING TO 60 MINUTES CORRESPONDENT LESLEY STAHL,
14TH NOVEMBER 2016

As Trump drives immigrants from their homes, there will be plenty of great deals on houses. Snap them up for a bargain. People fleeing for their lives generally take the first offer going, so make sure you really low-ball them. You'll be surprised at how little they're willing to settle for. Mexicans are great at cleaning, so snap up their houses first.

Same applies to household appliances such as TVs, Xboxes, laptops etc. You can drive an especially good deal on bulky white-goods, such as fridges and washing machines. Nobody wants to be encumbered by heavy appliances when they're on the run.

If the house has been abandoned, it's fair game

3. Go short on Europe

"European leaders gathered Friday to discuss a stunning about-face in the orientation of the United States, Europe's bedrock ally, amid fears that President Trump is seeking a breakup of the European Union."

— WASHINGTON POST, 3RD FEBRUARY 2016

Under the outgoing world-order, Europe had a role to play in building stuff, designing stuff and making nice jackets for us to wear.

Also, NATO was a great way for military officers to be able go on holidays to Europe.

Problem is, most Europeans, speak English with a heavy accent that is too annoying for Donald Trump to bother with.

As a result, Trump shares Vladimir Putin's desire to see the European project halted, and to return to the halcyon days of the 1910s – 1940s, when Europe became a net importer of many goods, especially armaments and ammunition. And if history shows us anything, it is when the United States and Russia gang up against Germany, they win!

Once Trump "wins" the election in 2020, expect Russia to get Ukraine back, and then much of the rest of Europe. Remember just like in 1945, Germany doesn't have the raw materials to win a major war of attrition. But the US and Russia do!

4. And Iran

"Nothing is off the table" in dealing with Tehran

— DONALD TRUMP, 5TH FEBRUARY 2017

5. And Asia

"If we have nuclear weapons why can't we use them?"

— DONALD TRUMP, 3RD AUGUST 2016

For too long, the United States has put up with erratic tinpot dictators having access to nuclear arms and threatening to use nuclear weapons. Now it's America's turn.

It's well known that Trump's son Eric, wishes to go to war with China. One way to do that would be through a proxy war in North Korea. But Donald has a soft spot for Kim Jong Un. Maybe some sort of bioweapon released in the middle of China's industrial belt. Who knows?

Sit back and enjoy. Just make sure you're far enough away to avoid the contagion.

6. Get your own offshore bank account

Mr. Trump said the U.S. dollar was already "too strong". "Our currency is too strong. And it's killing us."

— WALL STREET JOURNAL 17 JANUARY 2016

Be like an Australian Federal Cabinet member! Whether it's an anonymously numbered Swiss bank account, or a Cayman Islands shelf company, it's important in times of turmoil to spread the risk around.

Remember - not every major currency will survive the Trump administration, so you may wish to diversify into other asset classes that will have enduring value even if the monetary system completely collapses.

Do what Bob Katter has done, and safely stash away a few rods of plutonium, and you'll always have someone willing to barter food, shelter and protection for it.

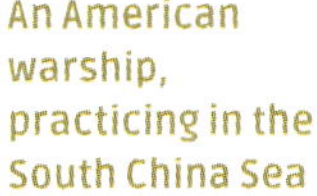

An American warship, practicing in the South China Sea

Pivot your business to make useful consumables like ammunition

7. Start making useful products

Since you're a winner, you probably own your own business, or at least inherited one.

If you're into any sort of high-tech start up that makes 'apps', stop what you're doing now, and pivot your company to produce goods that will be needed in the new geo-political environment.

Google - nobody wants some stupid service that allows you to search the internet, especially when nowadays they can get all their information on their Facebook feed. Wikipedia – your site is full of FAKE NEWS. Get a real job. Reddit – you're all LOSERS.

While the manufacture of ammunition may seem like a competitive playing field, the fact is that in times of uncertainty, national governments tend to source their ammunition from local factories, which means there really can never be enough.

The good thing about ammunition is that it's a consumable. If human nature is anything to go by, the demand for it will never run out.

If ammunition is not your style, then consider running a news site to compete with the FAKE NEWS outlets. Friendly reporting of @realDonaldTrump's tweets is a cheap and easy way to spin a dollar. If you become large enough, who knows, you may be seen as crucial to the administration.

8. Finally, make sure you keep up to date with Twitter feed

We must keep "evil" out of our country!

— @REALDONALDTRUMP

In any authoritarian regime, it's important to keep up to date with the latest obsessions of the leader. One minute he may be focused on being evil, next he wants to keep 'evil' out of the country.

If you don't keep a close eye on Twitter, you may well end up on the wrong side of an Executive Order. Trump changes his mind so often that taking a definite position on anything is risky.

The solution? Become a close relative of Trump. They're his only staff members who've managed to survive for any length of time. ★

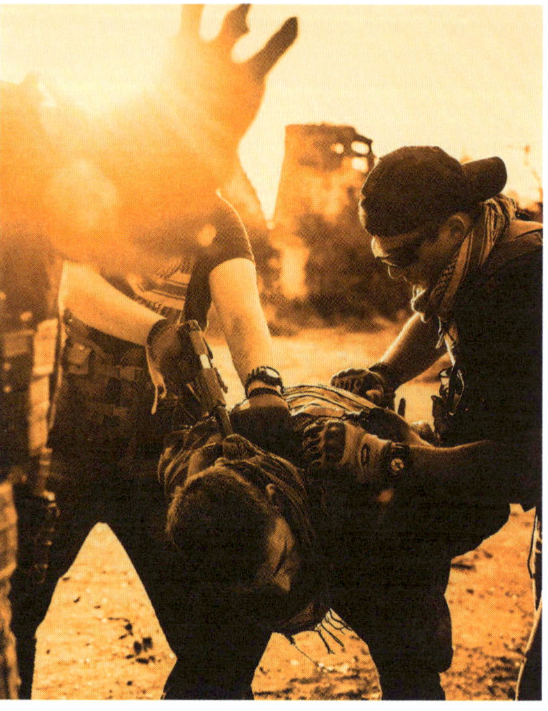

A citizen who did not keep up with Trump's Twitter feed gets taken away for 'questioning'.

LOSE 80 KILOS IN JUST 24 HOURS!

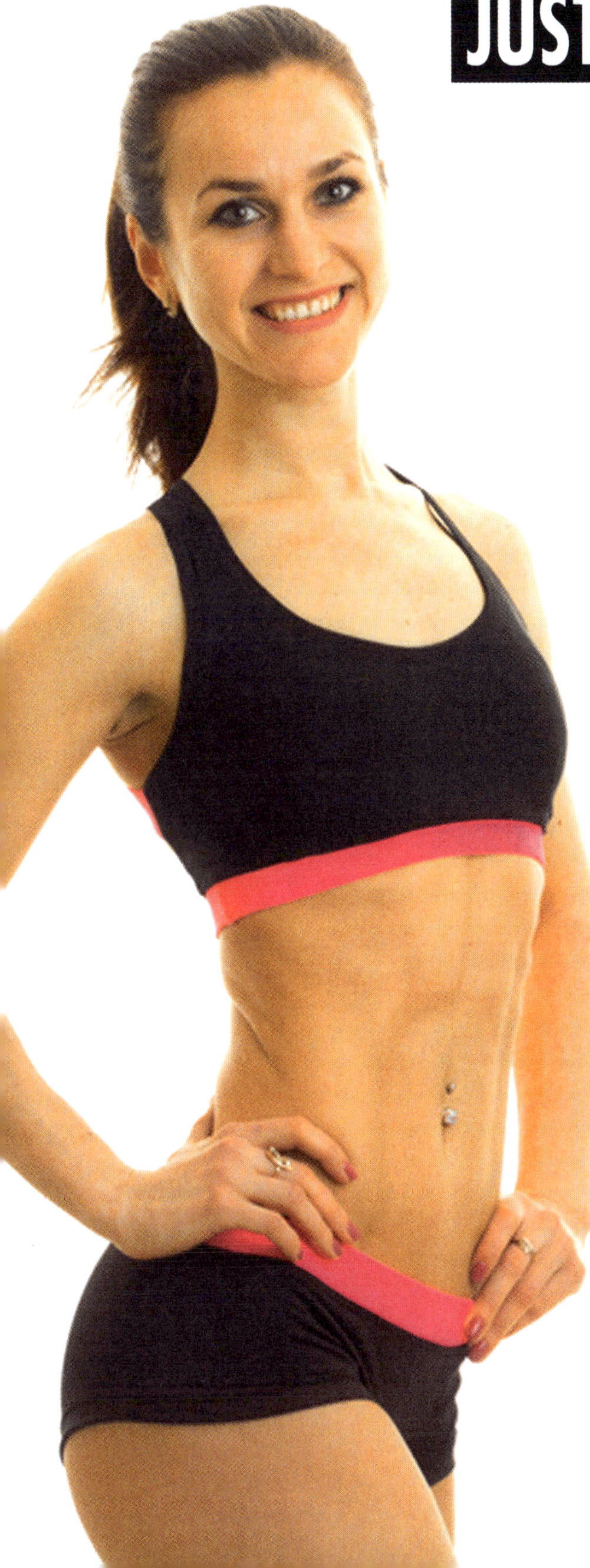

No weights
No jogging
No fad diets

"I lost over 90 kilos and I feel great!"
- Kelly

BECAUSE WE KNOW WHAT IT'S LIKE TO NOT WORK

UNEMPLOYMENT SUPPLEMENT

1,500mg

WARDS OFF HARMFUL ROBOTDEBT

FORTIFIED WITH SERPENTES OLEUM

GOOD SOURCE OF SUCROSE

BASED ON SCIENTIFIC & TRADITIONAL EVIDENCE

PREMIUM QUALITY FORMULA

VITEX (Vitex agnus-castus) extract equiv. dry fruit 1.5 g

WARNING: DO NOT SWALLOW

60 TABLETS A DAY

Why I'm an outsider

Life after politics hasn't always been easy for Mark Latham who has often struggled to make ends meet as a political commentator, newspaper columnist, and best-selling author. Yet despite his recent sacking from Sky News over homophobic comments regarding a schoolboy, the big man has bounced right back with the release of his new Facebook page, Mark Latham's Outsiders. **MARK LATHAM** describes his new project.

Mark Latham's Outsiders is a space where the marginalised and oppressed can speak out against the tyranny of the politically correct cultural Marxist freedom haters who have a stranglehold on this. Some of the dickbrained leftist retards in the media have the temerity to question my outsider status just because I'm a tertiary educated white man who was formerly opposition leader of the first world country in which I live. Well I can tell you now that I, and the enlightened people who agree with me, are tired of this rubbish. We are tired of watching from the fringes of society as the transgendered feminist immigrant brigade tears this country's heart out, chews it up and sneers at us through bloodstained teeth. We will not be silenced. We're outsiders, like Eminem in that song where he had to slice off a fat chick's nipple to stop her unwanted sexual advances. Except more so, because we don't have flick-knives to defend ourselves, only words. We've taken the red pill, put on the special sunglasses. Our eyes are open and we're not going to mindlessly obey and watch TV unless it's my new show.

As the founder of the Outsiders, I'm the outsider's outsider, a political pariah who plays by his own rules in a sea of conformist robots. I'm a patriot, a renegade, the Charles Bronson of the public speaking circuit who drives around at night with a cigarette dangling from his lips looking for those who have wronged me. Particularly cameramen. And taxi drivers. A women.

Sometimes when I'm giving a talk in front of a packed university auditorium it hits me with the force of an angry ex-politician crash tackling a cab driver to the ground, I think wow, I'm even more of an outsider than a vagrant who spends his life wandering around outside drinking methylated spirits and dying prematurely of liver cancer. The podium is symbolic of my lonely outpost.

As an outside, Mark Latham is shut out of the media (except for 2GB, Triple M, 2UE, 4BC and 2UE)

But now I have a new podium, a platform from which no one can sack or silence me. Or you, my fellow outsiders. We may be ridiculed in the press and vilified by the anti-white racists who throng the corridors of power. We may envy those who don't know how lucky they are to be out there in the sun tarring roads and lugging bags of wet cement up six flights of stairs on a construction site far from the flak and oblivious to our burden, but the struggle of we, the outsiders, will go on regardless of the toll. ★

Medical marvel

The hospital that replaced doctors with Google

Hailed as a triumph in alternative medicine, one hospital is leading a revolution in the delivery of medical services, by doing away with doctors, nurses and preconceived notions of what constitutes 'minimum standards of care'. **JAMES SCHLOEFFEL reports.**

Do you have the skills?

Not everyone is cut out to become a medical professional. To qualify you must be able to use Google, Bing and Ask Jeeves. A Reddit login also helps when you find yourself needing to gain advice from your peers.

Trust
With the widespread availability, trust in alternative medical treatment is soaring. 42% of Australians now trust the first result on Google over their GP.

»Jason Wells is lying on a bed in the emergency ward at Mt McInnes Hospital. His leg, severed in two by a chainsaw accident just hours earlier, is gushing blood onto the floor below. He's screaming in pain and losing consciousness fast. Luckily, Jason is in good hands.

You see, this is no ordinary hospital. A year ago Mt McInnes Hospital replaced all of its doctors with a team of stay-at-home mums who know their way around Google. Tech-savvy and up-to-speed on the latest search terms, the mums dial in each day to provide minute-by-minute instructions to the receptionists on the emergency ward floor.

The initiative has been hailed in alternative medical circles as a 'raging success', 'well overdue' and 'a triumph of common sense over entrenched elitism'. Not only has the hospital saved millions of dollars in doctors' wages, it's been relieved of vast amounts of dangerous science.

Of course, science is the last thing on Jason Wells' mind right now, as he has passed out from blood loss. What follows is a remarkable display of quick thinking, team work and some dazzling search engine skills.

While Jason is comforted by the hospital's receptionists, Laura Hughes (from her home in Endeavour Hills) Googles 'how to fix a severed leg'. She's lightning on her fingers, opening up dozens of links in new tabs as she expertly scans the search results, all the while providing a running commentary to the receptionists listening on speaker phone back at the hospital.

It's an impressive display. Within minutes, Laura has found a forum dealing with alternative techniques for lower-limb surgery, as well as a Facebook comment thread on natural disinfectants for amputation wounds.

"It's quite a skill," Laura, who has a Certificate IV in Picture Framing, later tells me. "When you have someone on the other end of the line losing blood and falling into hemorrhagic shock, there's no time to be distracted by clickbait or pop-up ads for handbags. You need to be able to focus on finding the right remedy, or range of remedies, and fast. Then you can look at the handbags. It's not for everyone."

I ask her if she feels qualified to do what she does. "Humbly speaking, yes. You probably know someone who, for some reason, is just better at Googling stuff than others? I guess I'm one of those people. Once,

When Jason Wells hurt his leg in a chainsaw injury, he turned his back on the entrenched elitism of the modern medical system.

for a friend, I found the artist's name and title for a song, based solely on the phrase 'put a ring on it.'

Laura says the weakness of traditional hospitals is their narrow-mindedness. "Doctors think the fact that they've devoted seven or more years of their life to medicine gives them some kind of special insight into the way the body works. But I've got a body too. We've all got bodies. Doctors aren't unique.

"It's just arrogance. I mean, I studied picture framing for 12 weeks, but that doesn't mean I'm not open to other people's opinions on what will make a painting pop."

She says doctors are sadly stuck in their ways and totally reliant on science. "They never consider a range of views, or look at a disease from different spiritual or cultural perspectives. It's crazy! What about my

Not so alternative anymore!

As more and more people wake up to the medical establishment's lack of progress over the past 100 years, they are turning to alternative sources of information.

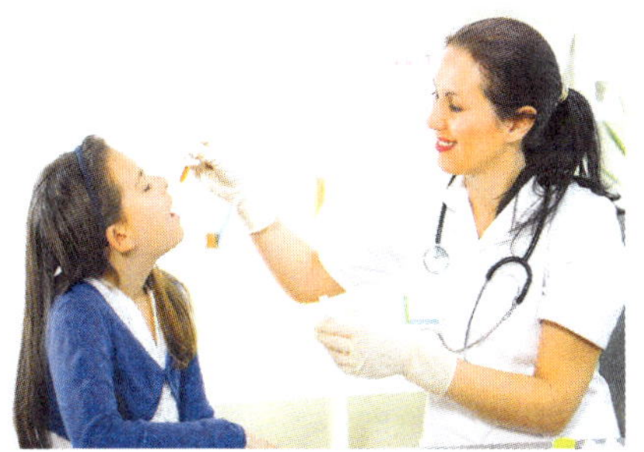

The great thing about homeopathic remedies is that they don't line the pockets of Big Pharma. Here, a nurse gives a girl with a lung infection a dose of Hog's Wart, diluted to one part per million. (The girl died of unrelated complications).

Medical breakthroughs can be implemented much faster when elitist 'clinical trials' are avoided. Here, a group of practitioners at Mt McInnes Hospital catch up on the latest treatments for cancer before making the rounds.

It's never too early to teach your child the basics of searching the internet. Here, a mother teaches her daughter how to remove hemorrhoids in middle-aged men.

BOOST FOR JOBS: Kelly Naylor, right, had been unemployed for five years before becoming the lead surgeon at Mt McInnes Hospital.

opinion? What about the opinion of Brad from Nimbin, posting on a natural health forum? Isn't that equally valid?"

Laura says that by 'democratising medicine' Mt McInnes Hospital has access to thousands of different views and opinions instantly. "When you think about it, it's amazing that anyone uses doctors at all anymore."

Back at the hospital, it's a hive of activity. "Elevate the leg," Laura shouts over the phone. The tone is abrupt, but professional.

"The attached or the unattached part?" one of the receptionists asks.

"Both."

The receptionist in question responds immediately, lifting Jason's leg parts above her head.

"Clean the wound with goose milk," Laura continues after a short pause. "Correction, goat's milk – sorry, misread that."

Another receptionist rushes to the medicine cabinet marked 'goat's milk' and grabs a two-litre bottle. He pours it liberally over the wound, while an assistant uses a coconut shell to collect the spillage.

There's a nervous wait. "Are we ready to operate, Laura?" one of the receptionists asks, after several minutes.

"Almost, I'm just watching a YouTube video on ancient Mongolian limb re-attachment methods. Stand by. It's playing one of those ads that you can't skip."

As the receptionists await their next instruction, the nervous energy in the room is palpable, but the next instruction will never come. The head receptionist confirms the worst. Jason Wells is dead.

As the muffled tones of the YouTube video's Mongolian soundtrack slowly fade out, a heaviness envelops the room. The receptionists go about their work in silence. One covers Jason's face with a sheet. Another picks up his lower leg, which has fallen to the floor.

Fewer complaints
Complaints by patients at the Mt McInnes Hospital plummeted an astounding 95% since it replaced doctors with Google. Not only that, its mortality rate has soared by 95% too. Whatever that is.

Much later, as the last pools of blood are cleaned from the laminate, news comes in as to the cause of Jason's death.

"He had an allergic reaction to some antibiotics his doctor prescribed for a skin infection last year," the head receptionist confirms.

"Bastards," someone mutters.

"Poisoned!" another hisses.

There's a sense of disappointment and of sadness. But mostly the mood, at both ends of the phone line, is one of anger.

"It's such an injustice," Laura tells me later. "What did this man do to deserve this?

"We see deaths like this all too often. Tumour patients dying from the carry-over effects of their chemo regimes or children coming to us with a broken leg and then dying from a finger infection they contracted from a toxic mass-produced bandage product."

While the death weighs heavily on Laura, she says setbacks like this come with the territory. "There's no time to get too sentimental. There's always another patient needing help."

In the four hours following Jason's death Laura will help deliver a child, provide advice on a four-year-old with measles, and talk receptionists through a tricky amputation for a woman with an incurable arm rash.

"It's stressful, I'm not going to lie. But it's very rewarding too. It feels good to know I didn't have to waste a decade of my life being brainwashed by Big Pharma and their poisonous beliefs. With just an internet connection, a search bar and a healthy dose of common sense, I can really make a difference – it's not brain surgery. Well, sometimes it is." ★

A practitioner at Mt McInnes Hospital shows a woman seeking contraception about the withdrawal method. She must have changed her mind because she is expecting her first child in September.

Health advice

with Dr. Google

So you're feeling fine. No need to panic right? Well before you go decide to just go on living your life, consider this horrifying statistic: almost ninety-five percent of people who report being 'fine' come down with a terminal illness within the next eighty years. Still think you shouldn't see a doctor?

Hi I'm Dr Google, and I'm here today to talk to you about why that occasional pain you get in your knee could be cancer.

Many people in society aren't aware of the symptoms of cancer, or are aware of the symptoms but aren't aware that sometimes cancer can have no symptoms at all. If you or anyone you know aren't suffering from the symptoms of cancer, please consult your GP for an immediate screening. There is a very high chance they may be about to die.

It's also important to consider that the lack of symptoms of cancer could also be indicative of a number of other fatal diseases, which could easily confuse a trained and experienced health practitioner into thinking you're fine. Diabetes, deep vein thrombosis, HIV, hysteria and the black plague are all known to sometimes present no symptoms, and it's very likely you are suffering from one or all of these diseases without even realising it.

'But what if I *am* showing symptoms of a disease Dr Google?' I hear you type. 'Does that mean I are actually not got disease?' No, my illiterate friend, in fact the situation is much worse. Not only are you now certainly at risk of secondary infections, but there is also the high probability that what you think is a benign cold is actually malaria. At this stage I would strongly suggest separating yourself from contact with children, adults, and society at large, and to begin calling for a hazmat team to dispose of your body.

Now you may not be entirely concerned about malaria because you've been immunised, but if that is the case I'm afraid I've got some even worse news. I've seen many highly cited internet blogs that claim that the malarial vaccine can cause death, autism or even malaria. This may seem hard to believe for a drug specifically designed to prevent the disease, but when it comes to information on medical research, how could a stranger on the internet be wrong?

That's all for me this week, but remember - next time you're feeling weak, nauseous, groggy, or fine, don't forget to check in with Dr Google for some unsubstantiated medical advice, just to be safe.

After all, what's the worst that could happen? Cancer? Probably.

BIG **SULTANA**

Last year 1,334 people died on Australian roads.

So why are you still feeding your child sultanas?

The science is in.
The correlation between people eating sultanas in early childhood and car crashes is now undeniable. But until the sick link between politics and sultanas is broken, the road toll will only continue mounting. JAMES SCHLOEFFEL has this special Chaser instigation.

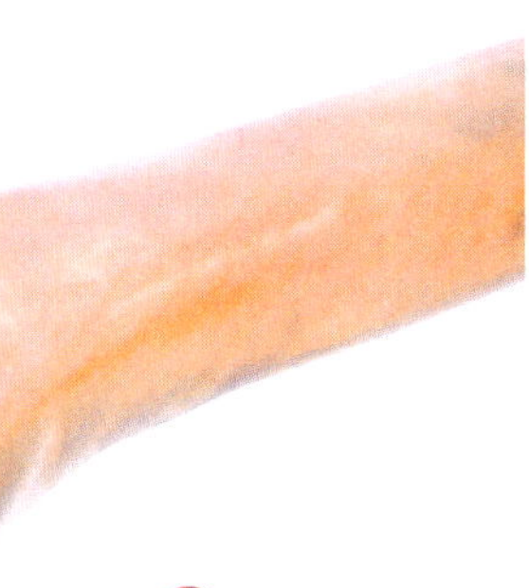

TOXIC. The statistics show there is no such thing as a safe dose of sultana. Consuming as little as one spoonful can lead to car injury, or even death, later in life.

The evidence linking toddler sultana consumption and car crashes later in life is overwhelming. A now-famous 2008 paper by Dr Rupert Horowitz found that of all car crash victims, 79% had eaten sultanas as a child. And it's getting worse. A more recent study suggests the percentage may now be above 85%.

Yet over the past 40 years Big Sultana has lined its pockets with billions of dollars in profits, cashing in on the naivety of Western parents and spurred along by a reckless media.

How do they get away with it? For decades now, Big Sultana has used sophisticated marketing techniques to obscure the link between these toxic snacks and auto accidents.

They've cleverly avoided all references to car crash deaths on their packaging, instead using highly stylised images of sultanas and misleading 'nutrition' information. Worst of all, they have tricked busy parents into thinking that boxed sultanas are a convenient and 'healthy' modern snack.

Convenient now maybe. But not so convenient in 20 years time when those same parents are called to identify the body of their dead son or daughter on the side of a rural highway.

Car tragedies are correlated strongly with sultana consumption in childhood

It's heartbreaking, but also infuriating to see a child naively eating a box of sultanas, knowing that they will almost certainly die in a traumatic car accident later in life.

Not convinced? Consider this. In the 1700s, before processed, boxed sultanas, there was not a single road fatality in Australia. Now there are over a thousand every year. A coincidence? Hardly.

Did you eat sultanas as a child?

Blackmores Anti-Sultana Extract is known to significantly reduce the sultana-induced toxins in your body that lead to car-crash deaths. A scientific mix of raisinmoxolin and nograpeadol, take six per day for the rest of your life for best results.

(Or, if you want to spend more money, try Blackmores Anti-Sultana Extract Ultra Boost. Same ingredients, just 40% more expensive.)

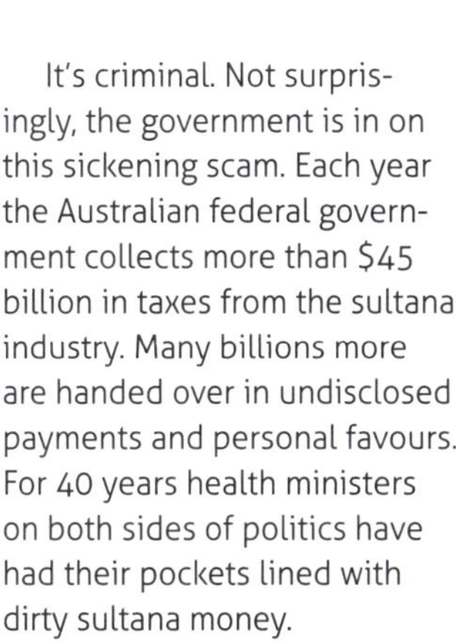

Here, a sultana-eater suffers an entirely preventable death. The question is who is protecting Big Sultana? And why does he only have one shoe on?

It's criminal. Not surprisingly, the government is in on this sickening scam. Each year the Australian federal government collects more than $45 billion in taxes from the sultana industry. Many billions more are handed over in undisclosed payments and personal favours. For 40 years health ministers on both sides of politics have had their pockets lined with dirty sultana money.

Don't believe it? Do your own research. Investigate, for example, the stringent regulations for packaging and advertising imposed on the cigarette industry and then ask yourself why the sultana industry gets off scot free.

The answer is obvious. The government knows that if each little sultana packet had an image of a blood-soaked body, impaled on a shard of windscreen glass, sales would plummet, and so would their backroom payments.

Instead, the government persists with its campaigns against drink driving and speeding, all the while obscuring the real cause of our shocking road toll – sultanas.

When confronted by the anti-sultana movement, Big Sultana simply denies a link with car accidents exists at all – even though documents prove they've known about it for decades.

> Each year the Australian federal government collects more than $45 billion in taxes from the sultana industry

When we interrupted a shareholder meeting by carrying in the coffin of a 38-year-old woman who had died in a car accident (surprise, surprise, she had eaten sultanas as a child) we were rudely asked to leave.

Last year when we broke into a sultana factory (with the blood of recent road trauma victims dripping from our hands) we were asked to cover up with gloves and hairnets. A neat metaphor for the cover up that has taken place in this industry for decades.

But it's the sultana executives who have blood on their hands. More than 700 road victims this year already. How many more before we say 'enough is enough'? It's time to wake up. It's time to do our own research, rather than relying on what's fed to us by lying sultana bosses. What they're feeding us is more than dried grapes in a box. They're feeding us certain death. ★

Superfood myth
Here a dangerously obese woman considers eating some lettuce, which is known to cause bloating, high cholesterol and overwhelms our digestive system.

Exclusive extract

The ultimate addiction: food

It's the diet craze that's taking over the world. More and more people are turning to Breatharianism. In an exclusive extract from her new book, nutritionist **BENDA KEATING** takes us through her journey to quitting food.

For most of my life, I never thought of myself as a quitter.

Not so long ago I was alone and struggling. Life took tremendous effort and my body was brought low with a lethargy that seemed impossible to shake. I'd begun walking across bridges late at night and gazing at the dark waters below. There had to be a better way.

I was teetering on the edge of one of those bridges when a little voice spoke to me.

"Let go of that deep-rooted resistance to quitting," it said.

ABOVE: No wonder I was feeling disgusting. My fridge used to be packed with toxins to which I was addicted, consuming them on a daily basis. RIGHT: My fridge now. Much better. (Please excuse my hideous, out of shape body).

It was coming from beneath the bridge. As it trailed off into the darkness (just before the splash) I heard these words:

"Quitting is forev –"

At that moment, I decided to quit. On my terms.

I'm going to share with you what I discovered.

I've developed an easy to keep to three-week plan. Along the way I'll explain the philosophy behind quitting, one by one the various food addictions that plague modern society. I'll show you that none of these are necessary. What we are aiming for is a pristine mind and body that thrives on pure air, sunlight and water, clear of all the toxins that plague modern men and women.

Back then, I was an addict who'd just had a revelation. I'd received a 'calling' from the universe.

As I researched it more in the following days, it became clear that all food was bad food. It impairs our defences and overworks our digestive systems. From a biological point of view, it's a harmful addiction that places a huge burden on our bodies.

As any detox must be carefully undertaken, I started mine slowly and methodically.

Day 1: I quit sugar

Who doesn't love the taste of toffee and the kilojoules in cola? My gut instinct had always been to guzzle. And who was I to query my gut? For years, I'd relied on 'feel' alone to govern everything below my tummy button.

As soon as I quit sugar, my mood disorders and sleep problems dissipated. I felt lighter and freer than I had in years.

Day 3: I quit Brussels sprouts

I didn't like them anyway, so that was easy.

Day 6: I quit gluten

Ask yourself, do you get an energy slump in the afternoon? Do you feel tired at bedtime? Do you need to evacuate your bowels every day? If the answer to any of these is 'yes' then gluten could be the culprit.

HARSH REALITIES

Sometimes, when you're quitting food, especially in the first few weeks, you might feel cravings. When your body has been bombarded with food for decades, it's only natural that it would become confused as it adjusts to a calmer, less onerous role. Push through. The cravings will fade as your body becomes accustomed to a new normal.

Day 7: Cold turkey on cold turkey

Every molecule we throw

Did you know? Breathing too much air is just empty kilojoules and can interfere with your attempt to shed the kilos. Try to finish breathing three hours before bedtime. Your metabolism slows down when you sleep but if you can hold your breath until morning, your metabolism will shut down completely, meaning no extra fat.

Don't quit quitting!
One of the best things about a Breatharian diet is that it cuts through many of the false debates in the dieting community. For example, with Breatharianism, it's not a matter of whether or not you should skip breakfast or not. Breakfast doesn't even exist!

down our gullets appeases an appetite hormone and it is with these that we must wage war. Meat, fish, poultry, dairy, grains and pulses were all strictly quarantined. I began to eat broccolini and only broccolini. Note: NOT to be confused with bocconcini.

Week 2: Cleansing
Next came two weeks of juice cleansing. I'd blend lawn cuttings with carbonated spring water to make a scrummy green shake. It looked a bit like bile but it tasted worse.

I thought of cleansing my liver. I read up on it but discovered that to do so, I'd have to eat liver, diced and fried, with or without bacon. As I'd already abandoned meat, I realised I'd have to reorder these simple steps to quitting before publication of my successful eBook.

Don't do it! Though you may be tempted to eat the occasional single pea, it's not worth it. Evolutionarily, our bodies were simply not designed to cope with food.

Week 2: The coffee loop 'hole'
I discovered coffee enemas. Within weeks I was packing a double macchiato mocha into the irrigator. I developed a very excitable personality AND I wasn't drinking coffee. Things were looking good.

I painted every wall in my house indigo and threw away all my LPs, aside from the Bruce Springsteen's *Greetings from Asbury Park, N.J.* I then scratched ley line chakras with a teaspoon, over all the tracks, except *Blinded by the Light.*

Some months later I was well on my way to being the man I'd always meant to be.

When Mum said, "I'm proud of you son, you're a quitter." I took a deep breath.

This praise had been a long time coming, but I'd missed lunch and was hungry for the kilojoules that only a big gulp of nature's finest can give.

Consider this:
Plants survive on air, light and water alone, so why can't humans?

Is Breatharianism for you?

Thanks to capitalism, your stomach is controlled by a powerful propaganda machine.

To become a breatharian you'll have to banish that sabotaging voice that is clamouring for food.

The Australian Breatharian Association recommends at least 23,040 breaths a day for a full calorific intake.

But remember don't gorge when you breathe. Gorging fills us up. Our body won't notice the excess in our system and it'll go undetected.

It's all about balance. Who ever heard of anyone dying from lack of breath? No one. But an excess can damage your health. Breathe easy and please be mindful – too much air can kill in the long term.

This woman greedily gorged on air. Luckily, she survived.

I was holding Mum's hand, for a final time, in the hospital, when she turned her face to me and said, "I'm so very proud of you son, you're a quitter just like me, just like your father, grandpop, your grandmop and your dearly departed and sorely missed sister."

For years, I dismissed my family's claim that it was possible to live only on air, sunlight and water, like a plant. As they all slowly wasted and shuffled off this mortal coil, I called them windbags and bid them riddance. But now I was not so sure.

Shortly thereafter I embarked on a life of total breatharianism. It had been staring me in the face all along. And I've never looked back. ★

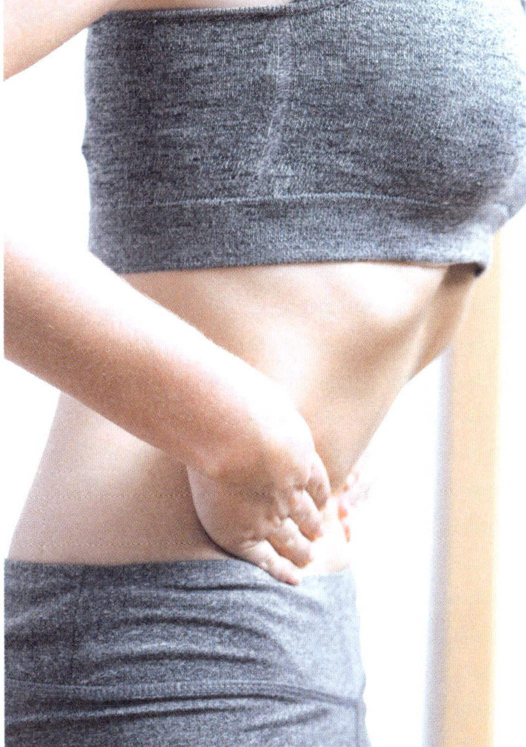

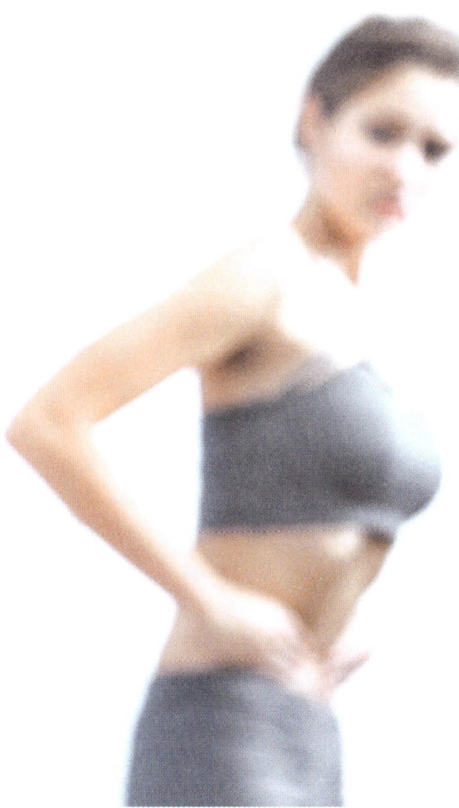

A photograph of me at the peak of my food addiction. Since then, I have lost 60kg.

Adani
Oil Action
Helps bleach those tough stains from your natural wonders

How to create your very own cult

Once upon a time being a cult leader was a shameful profession, limited to fringe religious movements, communist dictators, and the occasional aerobics instructor. But those days are long gone, and now it's not only acceptable, it's almost a requirement of business to be proficient in building a cult mentality in their customers.

Whether you're founding a startup that doesn't want to have to pay for sick leave, accruing millions of dollars by streaming videos of yourself playing video games in your bedroom, or simply entrapping your friends and family in a Tupperware based pyramid scheme - being able to convert your customers and clients into a mindless army of loyal followers is pretty much the first step in any business 101 course.

Step 1: Be hot

Gone are the days when the likes of Jim Jones and Bill Gates could become powerful cult leaders - today the field is crowded with thousands of hungry millenials and to stand out you're going to need an edge. You'll need to be charismatic. You'll need to be resourceful. And most of all, you'll need to be able to convince your followers to fork out $15 a month for access to the nudes in your OnlyFans account.

Step 2: Sell out

Sure a million people follow you on Instagram, but that's not going to pay the bills. A Silicon Valley cult leader is already syphoning off all the money generated by your free content, so you're going to need a second job, commonly known by modern cult leaders as a "side hustle". This can be all kinds of things, from promoting dangerous detox diets to your impressionable young followers, to rebranding a $12 Target makeup kit and selling it for $300, or even just starting a print publication to leech off the goodwill of fans of a long expired TV show.

Step 3: Lie

Lie about your products. Lie about your weight. Lie about your age. Hell, like about medical advice if it makes you money. Lie. Lie. Lie. Nobody likes real people, they're boring. What the people want is someone pretending to be real, while performing through the filter of 10 minor plastic surgery routines, facetune, and a dedicated lighting team. It's what we call the Gwyneth glow. And if you're running a startup you want to turn into a billion dollar product? Don't forget to tell investors about that hockey stick growth you know won't happen. Lies are the foundation of every great Silicon Valley business.

Step 4: Monetise your child

Need some funny content for your demanding millions of followers? Need to spice up an opinion on twitter that would just be sad if it didn't come from the mouth of a three year old? Or maybe you need a nice family photo to kick off the national listening tour you've organised to take the heat off that whole 'letting Russia steal the last election' thing. Whatever the cause, subjecting your children to the criticism of millions of people before they're even old enough to consent is a great way to manufacture a facade of authentic connection between you and your followers.

Step 5: Succumb to your conscience and walk away

So you've finally reached your dream, you're famous, you're successful, and you've made almost as much money as you would have made if you'd just finished that uni degree and then gone out and got a job. But you never realised running a cult would be so demanding. Turns out being obligated to interact with millions of people, 24 hours a day is not exactly conducive to sleep, or mental health. This is the point where you truly ascend to cult leader heaven, the ultimate grift. Tell your followers you are 'stepping back from day to day operations' to 're-assess your priorities' and then sell off the company/flog your most shameless coffee table book/start a GoFundMe and never return to the public spotlight again.

Step 6. Bank the dollars!

Dustin Hoffman reveals:

"I got vaccinated so I could properly portray the autistic side of Rain Man."

In new revelations, the Oscar winning actor reveals a commitment to his craft that has stunned Hollywood. **JAMES SCHLOEFFEL** reports.

Dustin Hoffman has never been one to do things by halves. For the 1982 movie *Tootsie*, Hoffman wore women's clothing for six months to prepare for the lead role. For *The Graduate* he had sex with older women for a year, before he even auditioned for the part. For *Rain Man* – the 1988 classic that won him an Oscar, he got vaccinated against tetanus just so he could contract autism.

It goes a long way to explaining why Hoffman's portrayal of the autistic savant,

Raymond Babbitt, was so convincing. It also explains why he never contracted tetanus on set. But mostly, it's yet another stark warning of the dangers of vaccinations.

Hoffman, who still has autism, wasn't able to give us an interview, but friends say it was a frightening transformation for the Hollywood star. "One minute he's the knockabout Dustin we all knew and loved, the next minute he's become socially awkward and really good at maths," says a family friend who doesn't want to be named.

She concedes *Rain Man* was a great movie, but says it wasn't really acting. "That was just Dustin being Dustin. He still thinks Tom Cruise is his brother."

Patricia Wintrero from the Anti-Vaccination Awareness Foundation says *Rain Man* is another sickening reminder of the power of the vaccination industry.

"They covered this up, and Hollywood was in on it too," she says.

"They said Hoffman was acting – they even awarded him for it. But it was clear to us at the time that this wasn't acting at all. Look at the evidence – his movies have been shit ever since," says Wintero.

Her message to aspiring actors? "A vaccination may get you an Academy Award. But it will get you autism as well."

Those on set at the time say Hoffman was among the most difficult actors with whom they had ever worked.

"He'd just walk onto the set, even when it wasn't his scene," one cameraman remembers.

"He would go on and on and on about Kmart or about some baseball game. On the plus side, when he accidentally stepped on a rusty nail one day, we didn't have any concerns at all about an infection. So that was good."

A director's assistant on the movie says Hoffman was basically a recluse.

"He didn't interact with the rest of the cast or crew, and he sat by himself at the lunch table. And then there was this weird thing he had about people not looking him in the eye. Actually, that was Tom Cruise, come to think of it," she said.

I ask Patricia Wintero from the Anti-Vaccination Awareness Foundation if it was possible that Tom Cruise had been vaccinated as well. "It's possible," she says. "Very possible. Those Scientologists certainly do believe in some crazy shit." ★

Cover up?

While the elites in Hollywood praised Hoffman's portrayal of an autistic man, others say it is just another sickening reminder of the power of the vaccination industry.

Hoffman's commitment to method acting means that, to this day, he still thinks Tom Cruise is his brother.

RAIN MAN: MONDADORI PORTFOLIO VIA GETTY IMAGES; AT OSCARS: KEVIN WINTER/GETTY IMAGES

My Day, with celebrity chef & Paleo diet guru, Pete Evans

With his Paleo diet empire going from strength to strength, we caught up with the ridiculously handsome Pete Evans and asked him to take us through his normal day as a modern day caveman.

5:23 AM Awoken by another drip from the roof of our cave as it slides slowly down my perfectly chiselled cheekbone and into my mouth. The roof leak irritates me but at least it's not fluoridated water. It's almost dawn. Time to hit the waves down at Maroubra. Which reminds me to check if cavemen actually rode surfboards? I hope so, or it undermines pretty much everything I stand for.

The Nutritional Mermaid is still slumbering peacefully on the dry side of the bed near the Locals Only graffiti. How come she never gets the wet spot?

5:45 AM Quickly scull a grass-fed steak tartare genuine free range egg yolk smoothie. The organic coconut oil is such a winning binder. Yummers. Leave a small glass of hemp milk with kale sprinkles at the bedside for N.M. There are several mutilated cat corpses in a pile near the cave mouth. She has been out hunting felines again. That's tomorrow's breakfast sorted.

6:01 AM Drive to Maroubra beach. En route there's another fucking nutritionist attacking me on the radio. The Paleo Way is nothing like Scientology. I'm much better looking than Tom Cruise.

6:25 AM Finally manage to pull on wetsuit. It's a little tight because Nutritional Mermaid suggested that one size too small would show off my pecs. Again, coconut oil came to the rescue. Brainwave new product: Paleo Organic Coconut Wetsuit Lube.

6:50 AM Ask fellow surfer to unzip me out of the wetsuit. Promise to autograph his in exchange. Surfed three sets together. Managed to catch a bream with my bare hands and rip its head off with my teeth. New mate reckons I'm a 'wild man'.

7:30 AM Back home to find the Nutritional Mermaid vacuuming the cave. I scold her for running the expensive Miele over the sandstone. Play 'scissors, paper, rock' to work out who cooks dinner. Mermaid wins again. Wonder from which of my many bestselling cookbooks I'll find tonight's meaty recipe?

9:10 AM Glance in the rear view mirror. Are my piercing blue eyes actually that blue? And the whites that white? Consider blowing myself a kiss but almost run up the back of a Hyundai Getz. My Hyundai Santa Fe would eat that Getz for breakfast, preferably with a rich bone marrow gravy.

9:22 AM Picked up the tux from the hire shop. I'm now all set for tomorrow night's award ceremony. The Bent Spoon Award will be another accolade in my blessed career; although I do remain confused, 'Australian Skeptics' is a bit of a dud name for a culinary organisation.

9:50 AM Still stuck in traffic heading for the studio. Manu Feildel texts me to say that he is already there. Smug French b'stard. How many global diet trends has he started, hey?

10:27 AM Producer implies that while they support me all the way on *My Kitchen Rules*, they'd like to keep a safe distance from outright advocacy of all the Paleo stuff. I consider bringing up the idea of danger money for all the processed crap I have to eat as a judge on this show. Instead I bite my tongue and discover it's made of meat. So I bite it again.

11:15 AM Email from TED saying they are thrilled with the viewing stats from the talk I gave at the Festival for Dangerous Ideas earlier in the year. My dangerous idea was that people should be able to eat their children if they already have enough. Most of the audience walked out. They aren't ready for quite this much danger yet.

12:33 PM Finalising travel arrangements for the U.S. The third season of The Paleo Way is going to be huge, largely because I'm a beautiful looking man. Take a phone call from Olaf at Malabar Roofing. The water main above our cave is responsible for the drips coming from the roof. In great alarm I ring the Nutritional Mermaid and warn her not to go near any of the fluoridated poison seeping from the cave roof. Complete coincidence that our teeth have a lot less cavities since we started drinking it.

.01 CAVEMAN

PREP TIME 10 million years | COOK TIME 6-12 h

DIRECTIONS

1. Place the chicken pieces in a stockpot. Add water, vinegar, sea salt, and leave to stand for – 1 hour.
2. Bring to the boil, continuously skimming of foam that forms on the surface of the liquid. S like you're stirring a potion in a cauldron. Red to low and simmer for 6 – 12 hours.
3. Perform Caveman voodoo dance. It helps wit
4. Store the broth in covered containers in your freezer. Not that refrigerators existed in cavema leave it out and if flies get into it think of it as ex

FROM THE KITCHEN OF ~~Neanderthal~~ Pete Evar

AmericanAirlines

BOARDING PA

12:47 PM Lunch. Californian free range organic grass fed turkey with wholesome free range organic Mullumbimby egg and organic basil mayonnaise and Belanglo bacon wrap.

2:01 PM Email from my co-writers of Bubba Yum Yum – Paleo Recipes for Babies. Charlotte has come up with a winning plan to capitalise on the current demand for baby formula in China. Chicken feet, liver and broth are already huge in China so if we dehydrate and package tonnes of it we'll make a motza, especially if my picture is on the tin. I've insisted that they go easy on the melamine. It's a Paleo no no.

YDNEY OPERA HOUSE AND ST JAMES ETHICS CENTRE PRESENT

FESTIVAL OF DANGEROUS IDEAS

BY FORMULA

VING 4 Litres	DATE 2.4 million years ago

INGREDIENTS

1.7kg bony chicken parts
2 – 4 chicken feet
500g chicken liver
2 tbsp. apple cider vinegar
Purified filtered water (from the lakes where dinosaurs used to drink and gather).

Optional for 6–8 months: mixed veggies such as celery, garlic, leek, carrots, pumpkin and sweet potato.

E ARE
GHANISTA
IE BANK
XUAL PERVERT

2:30 – 5:30 PM Filming. The audience hollers when I come on stage. Manu spits daggers. The contestants haven't got a clue. Get flustered when a jar of brown rice is spilt into the gravy and have to sit down. I assure the producer that I am not hyperventilating. A hex on grain and gluten!

5:45 PM I find a slot for the Hyundai near Darling Harbour and take the snips to the fence of Wildlife World. I promise the wombat that it'll be quick but the great fat hairy nosed thing bleeds out over my bare feet. I'm going to need a bigger cauldron back at the cave tonight.

Share your success stories
Have you got a success story about how homeopathy helped your health and well-being? If so, please drop an envelope describing your experience into the ocean, and by diffusion it should reach us via the water supply.

Homeopathy Word Search

A	B	C	D	E	F
G	H	I	J	K	L
M	N	O	P	Q	R
S	T	U	V	W	X
Y	Z	1	2	3	4
5	6	7	8	9	0
!	@	#	$	%	^
&	*	(	)	+	-
~	'	"	,	.	/

WORDS TO FIND: Every single word in the English language can be found in this word search, they are just extremely diluted. Nevertheless, we believe words can still be effective even if you only have 0.1% of the word, despite what so called "English language experts" might claim.